THE VĀKYAPADĪYAM

OF

BHARTṚHARI

BRAHMAKĀṆḌA

SRI GARIB DASS ORIENTAL SERIES NO. 146

THE VĀKYAPADĪYAM

OF

BHARTṚHARI

BRAHMAKĀṆḌA

English Translation

by

K. Subrahmanyam

Sri Satguru Publications

A Division of

INDIAN BOOKS CENTRE

DELHI - INDIA

Published by :
Sri Satguru Publications
Indological and Oriental Publishers
A Division of
Indian Books Centre
40/5, Shakti Nagar,
Delhi-110007
(INDIA)

First Edition : Delhi, 1992

ISBN 81-7030-328-1

Printed in India

Contents

Preface

The work is styled 'Vākyapadīyam' since it deals with sentence and word. There are three Kāṇḍas in this book :

1. *Brahmakāṇḍa :* It is also called Āgamkāṇḍa/Āgamasamuccaya. The identity of Śabda and Brahma, the authority of Vedas, attaining Mokṣa are chiefly discussed in this chapter. It consists of 156 verses.

2. *Vākyakāṇḍa* : The definitions of a sentence, discussions related to the definitions, theories of other systemists, indivisible sentence and its meaning, Vākyasphoṭa as the very Śabda, the defects of Padavādins etc. are discussed in this chapter, in about 487 verses.

3. *Padakāṇḍa (or Prakīrṇakāṇḍa)* : There are 14 Samuddeśas (sub-chapters) in this Kāṇḍa. Each Samuddeśa deals with a different subject and the total number of verses is 1323. Here-under is a break up :

1. Jātisamuddeśa (106 verses) 2. Dravyasamuddeśa (18) 3. Sambandhasamuddeśa (88) 4. Bhuyodravyasamuddeśa (3) 5. Guṇasamuddeśa (9) 6. Diksamuddeśa (28) 7. Sādhanasamuddeśa (167) 8. Kriyāsamuddeśa (64) 9. Kālasamuddeśa (114) 10. Puruṣasamuddeśa (9) 11. Samkhyāsamuddeśa (32) 12. Upagrahasamuddeśa (27) 13. Liṅgasamuddeśa (31) 14. Vṛttisamuddeśa (627). The subject matter in each Kāṇḍa can be summarised as follows :

1. *Brahmakāṇḍa* : At the end of this chapter the following sentence is read : iti śrīharivṛṣabhamahāvaiyākaraṇaviracite vākyapadīye āgamasamuccayonāma brahmakāṇḍam samāptam. Therefore, it can be presumed that Brahmakāṇḍa and Āgamasamuccaya are the names of the first part of Vākyapadīya.

In verses 24, 25 and 26 of Brahmakāṇḍa the author gives the gamut of things that are going to be discussed in the entire work. They are : 1. Prakṛtipratyayas 2. Padavākyas 3. Prakṛtipratyayārthas 4. Padavākyārthas 5. Kāryakāraṇabhāva 6. Yogyatā 7. Arthajñāna and 8. Dharma.

All the said eight things are described in three Kāṇḍas. One of the purposes, i.e. Dharma, is useful in attaining Mokṣa or Brahmaprāpti. This concept is predominantly proposed in the first part and hence the name Brahmakāṇḍa. Pratyaya or Arthāvagati or Bodha (conception of meaning) is the other purpose which is also mentioned in Brahmakāṇḍa.

Another name for Brahmakāṇḍa is Āgamasamuccaya. Some scholars feel that it is unmeaningful. The word 'Āgama' is used in the sense of conventional knowledge, Veda, Śāstra etc. and hence, others argue, the name is meaningful. From verse 133 onwards the author briefly discussed the authority of Āgamas, Tarka, Vedas etc. Therefore, it won't be amiss to call Brahmakāṇḍa, Āgamasamuccaya.

For Vaiyākaraṇas, Dharma is more important than Pratyaya. Dharma has got its origin in Vedas. Veda, itself is Śabdabrahman. Through Vyākaraṇa, which is one of Vedāngas, the speaker would distinguish between a Sādhu-Śabda and Asādhu-Śabda. Brahmaprāpti is possible only through the usage of Sādhu-Śabdas. Those, who think that the conception of meaning is the only purpose of the study of Vyākaraṇa, can have the knowledge of both Sādhu-Śabdas as well as Asādhu-Śabdas. Conception of meaning is possible through Asādhu-Śabdas too. The day to day transactions in the world won't be affected by the usage of Asādhu-Śabdas.

The concept of Sphoṭa is elaborated in verses 44 onwards. Bhartṛhari says that Sphoṭa is the real Śabda and it is different from Nāda and Dhvani and Vaikhary, which is born out of the movement of speech organs has got sequence and is unreal. These ideas will be elaborated under 'Sphoṭa'.

The second part of the treatise is called Vākyakāṇḍa. Sentence and its related matters – only Vākyārtha is real, Padas and Padārthas are artificial, the definitions of sentence and their evaluation establishing the Vyākaraṇa-view point – are discussed in this chapter. In case one argues that the Padas (words) attained through 'Apoddhāra' (extraction) of a sentence are meaningful then the Varṇas (phonemes) attained through splitting of Pada must also be meaningful. It is not happening-some words cannot be split, some others, when split, the parts thereof won't express the meaning that is there in the word and therefore they are 'dyotakas' (illuminators) and not Vācakas (expressers/tellers). Thus the entire chapter is earmarked for the discussions related to sentence.

The third part of Vākyapadīya is called 'Padakāṇḍa'. The words extracted from a sentence, different types of words, their relations with meaning are the subject matter of this Kāṇḍa. In the beginning it is stated that there is difference of opinion about the number of types of words-two, three, four and five. Among the words Nāma (noun) and Ākhyāta (verb) are important. So before he ventured upon the explanation of meaning of Nāmas and their place in a sentence, the author elaborated six things, viz. Jāti, Dravya, Sambandha, Bhūyodravya, Guṇa and Dik. In seventh Samuddeśa the author elucidates the instrumentality of Nāmas, which is the criterion in the generation of Kriyā (action) and which is originated from the power that the Nāmas possess. Since Vākyārtha (the indivisible sentence meaning) is the real factor and its base is the Kriyārthavyāpāra (the activity/process, which is the meaning of a verb), the instruments of Vyāpāra, called Kārakas have been detailed. The description of the form of Kriyā follows. The difference between Nāma and Dhātu, nature of Kriyā and the definition of Kriyā that-the parts having sequence would turn into a single unit without any differences in the mind and the same is called Kriyā-are elaborated. Next comes the Kālasamuddeśa, in which the form of Time (Kāla) is elucidated. The Present, Past and Future tenses alongwith the eleven sub-forms are explained. Puruṣasamuddeśa consists of Prathamamadhyamottamapuruṣas in detail. In Saṁkhyāsamuddeśa the questions related to Saṁkhyā (number) such as what is Saṁkhyā ? where does it exist ? how the separation of difference and non-difference (bhedābhedavibhāga) is regulated by Saṁkhyā ? – are discussed. Ātmanepada etc. are dealt at length in twelfth chapter called Upagrahasamuddeśa. Liṅgasamuddeśa chielfly deals with the difference between Laukikaliṅga (the gender in the world) and Śāstrīya-liṅga (the gender in Vyākaraṇa). The last chapter is Vṛttisamuddeśa. It consists of 627 verses. The Kṛt, Samāsa etc. Vṛttis and sub-differences thereof are discussed from different angles.

THE VĀGVYĀPĀRA (SPEECH PARLANCE)

The Śabda, that is useful in the expression of meaning, is of two types. – Dhvani and Sphoṭa (VP 1-44). The Śabdas of the speaker are the cause. They manifest the Sphoṭa, which is real, original and meaningful. (The word 'Śabda' is an untranslatable term used to denote-phoneme (Varṇa), morpheme (prakṛti/pratyaya), word (Padam), sentence (Vākyam), discource (Mahāvākyam), Sphoṭa, Vaikhary, ordinary sound, and Śabdapramāṇa). The Sphoṭa theory is a difficult subject. It's a mixture of Vyākaraṇa and Vedānta concepts. Vedāntins, like other systemists, do not accept the Sphoṭa-theory. Vaiyākaraṇas argue that since all the Varṇas cannot exist at a point of time, i.e. by the time the last phoneme is uttered, the earlier ones disappear and hence there must be something which helps in the understanding of the meaning of a sentence, and that is Sphoṭa. The speaker utters the Śabda with the help of speech organs and the same is heard by the listner. Such a Śabda is called Vaikhary. Other systemists call this Śabda and hold that it perishes in the next moment. The Vaiyākaraṇas hold it differently – it is not simply the movement of speech organs and the air that is happening at the time of speech-utterence. Rather, it has got certain sequence and it is capable of rendering some meaning that is desired by the speaker to express and such a Dhvani only is called Śabda. So much so that such a Śabda should have existed in the mind (buddhi) of a speaker before the speech-process has started. It is in the form of 'Madhyamā' and the same exists before the Vaikharydhvani has come out of the speaker's mouth. Consequently, such a Madhymā Śabda, mixed with the Bhāvanā (imagination) of meaning must have existed. We can know through examination that there are many Śabdas in our mind but not heard outside. Therefore, earlier to Madhyamā Śabda, there is another form of Śabda, where the Śabda and Artha are inseperable. It is called Paśyantī. Is it meaningful or unmeaningful ? It means 'looking'. What/who is looking ? Speech itself. The same is the Subject. When we see a particular thing like a house and identify the same, it is only through Śabda. On the other hand, let us suppose, we do not know its name. We may have the cognition and experience but they won't suffice to express our idea or help us to remember the thing.

As soon as we come to know the name of such a thing, immediately the association of Śabda and Artha takes place as well as the identity (Tādātmya). From then onwards we understand the thing through that name. The same is speech (Vāk) and the same is Paṣyantī. The one which is there in between Paśyantī and Vaikhary is Madhyamā. It means the middle one'. What is the difference between Paśyantī and Madhyamā ? – In Paśyantī-form Śabda and Artha are mixed and identical. In Madhyamā-form both have separate identity. For example – the Śabda 'cow' denotes both Śabda and Artha. If someone asks 'write cow' – either the word 'cow' can be written in script or the form of a cow can be sketched. Which one of the two things, i.e. the Śabda or the Artha (form) is meant by the Śabda is there clearly in Madhyamāvāk, in the mind of the speaker. In Paśyantīvāk they are in mixed form. Therefore, any Vāk (speech), one has to accept, has got all the three forms (VP 1-143). Another doctrine holds that a Śabda, which has got the earliest form which is there in the case of the mind and which is solid, called 'Parā' is there. Bhartṛhari speaks of this Vāk in verses from 112 to 115, Brahmakāṇḍa. The innermost Jñāta (knower) i.e., Jīvātmā, who is there in the form of minute speech gets the vivarta-form in order to manifest itself as a Śabda. Nāgeśa says that Parā is situated at Mūlādhāra-cakra, Paśyantī at Nābhi (Navel) Madhyamā in Hṛdaya (mind), and Vaikhary in the throat (Kaṇṭha). Bhartṛhari touches 'Parārvāk' in verses 17 and 18 of

Brahmakāṇḍa (see commentary). The famous hymn of Ṛgveda, i.e., Catvāri Vākparimitā Padāni... also supports the view of four-fold speech. The Vaikharyvāk can be considered to have fulfilled its task only after it enters the listner's ear in the form of atoms and brings out the meaning, which was already existing in his mind, in the form of samskāra, into the state of understanding-this is also called Vāgvyāpāra (the process of speech). A similar state of Śabda and Artha, which is eternal, is there in the form of recollection (Smṛti) or understanding (Avagati). Smṛti is where it was already known. Avagati, where it is a new one. Neither can be possible if the listner does not already have the Samskāra of Vācya (the denoted) and Vācaka (the denotor). The movement of atoms of Vaikhary śabda would manifest the eternal and indivisible Śabda and Artha, which are there in the mind of the speaker and enter the Buddhi (mind) of the listner in order to convert into an indivisible cognition (Akhaṇḍajñāna) – this is the manifestation of speech (Vāgabhivyakti). Therefore, Śabda is neither born nor perished – as it is in regard with Naiyāyikas, The Śabda, which is there both at the beginning and the end of speech-manifestation is eternal. The same is Sphoṭa. It is not Kārya (non-eternal). According to the Upādhi (resort) the Sphoṭa can be of three types-Vākyasphoṭa, Padasphoṭa and Varnasphoṭa (VP1-148 Vṛtti).

The following may be noted-The Pasyantīvāk (labdhānusamhārasvar ūpa), which is there in the mind of the speaker is the cause. Then its effect, called Vaikharyvak will be the Kārya (effect). The cause comes first and then the effect. Whereas in the case of the listner Vaikhary is the cause and the effect is the indivisible Vākyārtha (sentence-meaning) that is in his mind-this is the idea behind Bhartṛharis' usage of the two important attributes, i.e., 'kramavān' and 'akramanimittam', in regard with Śabda. The cause and effect in the case of the speaker (Vaktā) would appear in the form of effect and cause, respectively in regard with the listner (Śrotā). The result would be in the following order. Vaktā – Paśyantī – Madhyamā, Vaikhary – Madhyamā – Paśyantī – Śrota. Bhartṛhari wanted to give a clear picture of the sambandha between Vaikhary and Madhyamā and vice versa from the point of view of both the speaker as well as the listner.

SPHOṬA

All the Vaiyākayaṇas have accepted that there is an entity called Sphoṭa and it's the origin of all Śabdas, and therefore they became famous as Sphoṭavādins. Difference of opinion is noticed among Mīmāmsakas, Naiyāyikas, Vedāntins, Bauddhas, and Cārvākas. The roots of Sphoṭa-theory were already there in ancient times, rather Bhartṛhari can be considered to be the first to elaborate, propegate and accentuate the theory. The famous Mīmāmsaka, Kumārilabhaṭṭa and the Naiyāyika of similar fame, Vācaspatimiśra have vehemently refuted the concept. In his work 'Sphoṭasiddhi', Maṇḍanamiśra strongly advocated the theory of Sphoṭa.

It is important to know as to what Patañjali and Bhartṛhari have said about Sphoṭa, in order to understand the nature of Sphoṭa. The following is the discription of the nature of Śabda given by Patañnjali in Paspaśāhnika of Mahābhāṣya – "Then what is Śabda ? By the articulation of which an entity of concrete form, with dewlap, tail, hump, hoofs and horns is felt that is the Śabda, 'gauḥ']. In daily life the sound is reffered to as Śabda – that's how-make noise, do not make noise, this boy is making noise – are some usages, so Dhvani is Śabda. Similarly, Sphoṭa is Śabda. Dhavni is the attribute of Śabda. How ? Like the stroke on a drum. The sound (Dhvani) of a stroke travels upto twenty feet, that of another thirty feet, still another forty and so on. In the same manner Dhvani too. On the other hand Sphoṭa remains unchanged. The increase was due to Dhvani". It means that in this context Śabda and Sphoṭa are used as synonyms. The following may be an acceptable discription of the said three things – be it meaningful or meaningless, the activity of speech by a person is called Śabda. Dhvani is there in all the Śabdas. Does Sphoṭa exist in all Dhvanis ? – is not clear. If so, do Śabda and Sphoṭa have got equal pervasion (samānavyāpti) in meaning ? Don't they have any difference in nature ? Patañjali simply differentiated between Sphoṭa and Dhavani. (These doubts are clarified by the later commentators).

In the course of time, the popularity of Mahābhāṣya in North has gradually diminished. Then, says Bhartṛhari, with the help of the knowledge of Vyākaraṇa, he acquired through Candrācārya and Vasurāta, he wrote Vākyapadīya. While discussing many things, Bhartṛhari, elaborated the Sphoṭa-Theory. It is labored in verses – 44-49, 75, 77, 81, 93, 97, 102, 103 and 106 in Brahmakāṇḍa. Here is the gist of the ideas embedded in the above verses-of the two kinds of meaningful Śabdas, either is Sphota and it seems as if it is following the line of Nāda.

The time and sequence of Vaikṛtadhvanis are attributed to Sphoṭaśabda. The Prākṛtadhvani, in the form of Sphoṭa is the cause in the conception of Śabda. Those which follow are Vaikṛtadhvanis. Change (Vikāra) can be there only in Vaikṛtadhvan is and never in Prākṛtadhvanis.

Three-fold opinion is noticed regarding Sphoṭa – 1. Both, Sphoṭa and Dhvani are conceived as a single thing (identified with each other) 2. Only Sphoṭa is conceived and never Dhvani. 3. Dhvani is separately conceived. Sphoṭa can be taken as a class (Jāti), which occurs in many individuals (Vyaktis). Sphoṭa is suggested and Nāda (Dhvani) is suggestive. Sphoṭa is the result of the union and seperation of speech organs and efforts (Sthāna and Karaṇa). Those born out of Sphoṭa and those which follow it are Dhvanis. According to this theory the Sphota is momentary (Kṣaṇika).

Let Dhvani be short or long, the Sphoṭa does not change. The whole gamut of Śabdas (Dhvanis) born out of Sphoṭa can be more or less. It can be deduced, depending on the above analysis of Bhartṛhari, that during the course of his time itself there were different opinions regarding the form of Sphoṭa among Vaiyākaraṇas. They were arguing that Sphoṭa was eternal and non-eternal, different and non-different from Dhvanis. The adversaries of Vaiyākaraṇaś, i.e. Mīmāmsakas and Naiyāyikas did not embrace the Sphoṭa-theory. Knowing pretty well that the Vaiyākaraṇas, having taken Union with Brahman (Brahmaikya) from Advaitasiddhānta and having accepted the identity of Sphoṭa with Brahman, were advocating Advaita, Śankarācārya (in Devatādhikaraṇa of Śankara-Bhāṣya on Brahmasūtras) has criticised Sphoṭa.

Patañjali, in Mahābhāṣya emphasized the identity of Sphoṭa and Śabda (Sphoṭaś śabdaḥ). He rather indicated three significant attributes of Śabda – 1. Capacity to render the meaning (Arthabodhakatva), 2. having sounds (Dhvanitva) and 3. Sphoṭatva, but did not elaborate the Sphoṭa.

In fact, the Sphoṭa and its nature can be, like that of Brahman, discerned only by siddhas. That'swhy it is described as Śabdabrahman. On the other hand, it is generally accepted that Śabda, in the form of waves, pervades the space (Ākāśa). The waves are eternal (like a stream-Pravāhanitya) and it is identical with Brahman. In the creation of such waves there must be, like the stroke of a drum, some cause. The need is fulfilled by Sphoṭa. Bhartṛhari advocated identity of Sphoṭa with Brahman. During the course of time, the commentators of Mahābhāṣya have elaborated the Sphoṭa-theory. Such a Sphoṭa is of eight types – 1. Varṇasphoṭa, 2. Padasphoṭa, 3. Vākyasphoṭa, 4. Akhaṇḍapadasphoṭa, 5. Akhaṇḍavākyasphoṭa, 6. Varṇajātisphoṭa, 7. Padajātisphoṭa 8. Vākyajātishoṭa.

Sāyaṇācārya, the author of Sarvadarśanasamgraha, was of the following view—'Bhartṛhari says that the eternal Śabda, which was the origin of the Universe and called Sphota, itself is the Brahman. Mammaṭa, the author of Kāvyaprakāśa, says that the suggestive Śabda (Vyañjakaśabda) of the chief-suggested-meaning, which is in the form of Sphoṭa is styled Dhvani by Vaiyākaraṇas.

PRĀKṚTADHAVANIS AND VAIKṚTADHVANIS

During the course of discussion the Vaiyākaraṇas use the following Śabdas—Śabda, Sphoṭa, Dhvani (Vaikṛtadhvani and Prākṛtadhvani), Parā, Paśyantī, Madhyamā and Vaikhary. The Advaita school of Philosophy advocates that the names and forms may be different as in the case of gold (it is gold only, whether it is in the form of bullion, or polished, unfinished/finished ornament) but everything in the universe is Brahman. Similarly, the Śabda in the form of Sphoṭa, which is there in the individual is given so many names listed earlier. So Bhartṛhari employed the word Śabda many times in several meanings in his work. There would be some ambiguity and delay in understanding and depending on the context etc. one has to decide the meaning.

What is the difference between Dhvani and Śabda ? Dhvani is that which is there in the individual and employed in the form of movement of speech organs in order to express some meaning. The Dhvani is the cause and suggestive of the idea, which was there earlier. There is a doubt—Sphoṭa is said to be eternal and indivisible and hence there should not be differences like—hrasva, dīrgha, udātta, anudātta and svarita-in a Sphoṭa, then how all these things are there in Sphoṭa ?—In fact, the differences which are there in the Dhvanis are attributed to Sphoṭa. Here is a simili-we notice the reflection of Moon in a sheet of fresh water. When there is disturbance on the surface of the water, the same is felt in the reflection also. Similarly, all the attributes/virtues, that are found in Dhvani are superimposed in Sphoṭa, which otherwise, has got no other forms. The Dhvanis (that were immediately after Sphoṭa) pronounced are called Prākṛtadhvanis. Those which follow the same are called Vaikṛtadhvanis. The attributes are those noticed in Prākṛtadhvanis.

The following question may be asked—How to identify between Prākṛtadhvanis and Vaikṛtadhvanis ?—Prākṛtadhvani is that without which the Sphoṭaśabda (unmanifested) cannot be analysed. Vaikṛtadhvani is that which makes available the manifested-Sphoṭa for some time (through waves) uninterruptedly. So much so that, it can be concluded that the Prākṛtadhvani is that which is produced through the speech organs (at the place of speech organs). In the stable air, which is there beside the Prākṛtadhvani, the second wave is produced (anuraṇana). Only both of these are called Prākṛtadhvanis. That is the later waves, called Vaikṛtadhuni, which reach the listner and manifest the meaning (Śabda syordhvamabhivyakteḥ – Bhartṛhari, and anuraṇanarūpā ye paścātbhāvinaḥ-Helārāja). This process is akin to the Propegation of Sound (Radio waves) developed by Physicists in modern times. The Indian Phylosophers (apart from Bhartṛhari etc., Viśvanāthabhaṭṭācārya, author of Bhāṣāparicchcda and Dharmarājādhvari, author of Advaitaparibhāṣā) have advocated that sound travels in two ways – 1. Vīcītaraṅganyāya (like waves) and 2. Kadambamukulanyāya (like the shape of the bud of a Kadamba-Nauclea Cadamba a tree with fragrant orange-colored blossoms, i.e. in all ways). The verses of Vākyapadīya were referred to by many authors of different schools-Kṣīrasvāmī (commentator of Śatapathabrāhmaṇa 638 AD), Jayantabhaṭṭa (Nyāyamañjarī, 880 (AD), Rāmakaṇṭha (Vṛtti on Skandakārikā 950 AD), Somānandanātha (Śivadṛṣṭi, 970 AD), Mādhavācārya (Sarvadarśanasaṃgraha, 1350 AD), Śāntarakṣita (Tattvasaṃgraha, 720 AD), Kamalaśīla (Tattvabindu, 820-900 AD), Bhavya (Prajñāpradīpavṛtti, 600 AD), Gokulanātha (Padavākyaratnākara & Śivasūtravṛtti), Bhojarāja (Śṛṅgāraprakāśa) etc. have touched the ideas of Bhartṛhari. Kaiyaṭa, Bhaṭṭojidīkṣita, Kauṇḍa-Bhaṭṭa, Nāgeśa etc., propegators of Vyākarana theories have quoted extensively from Vākyapadīya.

Contribution of Bhartṛhari

Patañjali, who was an erudite scholar in all the systems of Indian Philosophy, has put the gems of Vyākaraṇa-theories in a nutshell, called Mahābhāṣya (It is Mahabhāṣya and not simply Bhāṣya because one can find the origin of most of the theories related to all the Śāstras in it).

In the course of time, the people in North, who had poor intelligence could not keep up and protect the tradition of Mahābhāṣya. Candrācārya somehow secured a copy from South and tought to his descipie, Vasurāta and Bhartṛhari got it from him. Vākyapadīya is the gist of the theories of Mahābhāṣya. Bhartṛhari's contribution can be summarised as follows –

1. The Sphoṭasiddhānta, which is there in Mahābhāṣya, in the form of a seed is elaborated in many ways by him.

2. Darsanas like Vedānta were advocating ways of attaining Mokṣa etc. during his lifetime, whereas Vyākaraṇa was considered as a tool in knowing the form of Śabdas. In such a situation he ventured upon the task of proving that Vyākaraṇa too is a Darśana and it's verily useful for Mokṣa, rather it is like a royal path (Ajihmā rājapaddhatiḥ).
3. He advocated the identity of Śabda with Brahman and argued that the entire Universe is in Śabdabrahman.
4. He elucidated the concept of Patañjali that through the employment of Sādhu-Śabdas one would know the real form of Veda and thus get on the track for attaining Dharma (this point is criticised by Somānanda in Śivadṛṣṭi).
5. Taking the idea that Omkāra emerged first at the beginning of creation from Upaniṣads he propegated that Vāk is Anādi (beginningless) and is the origin of the Creation.
6. He refuted the theories of other systemists, which were in vogue during his life time.
7. He established the Vaiyākaraṇas' Akhaṇḍavākyārtha, after having refuted vehemently the concepts of Naiyāyikas and Mīamsakas.
8. He construed the Vaiyākaraṇasiddhāntas alongwith Advaitavedānta and Vedaprāmāṇikatva (authority of Vedas). He brought Sphoṭa on a par with Apūrva of Mīmāmsakas, Īśvara of Naiyāyikas, Pīlu of Kaṇādas, Śūnya of Bauddhas and Brahman of Vedāntins.

Several translations of Vākyapadīya-Brahmakāṇḍa are already available. Nevertheless, there is a fresh demand for a more faithful and exhaustive rendering of the same work. Therefore, I have taken up the task of preparing a rendering afresh, i.e. each verse is preceded by an Introduction and followed by Summary, Commentary and Notes. I earnestly hope that this pattern would certainly be useful to the readers in having the related poient of material of each verse at a single place. It is my belief that one need not go to *works* related to other Systems/Schools in order to understand the points touched by the author at different places. The explanation of each verse, on the whole, is akin to the one rendered to a *śiṣya* by a Guru in the traditional way. With the experience I gained during the course of my study of different Śāstras alongwith Veda in Gurukulas, I tried my best for greater clarity of the text and it is for the readers to judge whether I could succeed in my endeavour.

1

Vākyapadīyam-Brahmakāṇḍaḥ

Introduction

According to the tradition, the author of every treatise must indicate the so called Anubandha-catuṣṭaya, viz. 1. Subject, 2. Purpose, 3. Relation and 4. the Qualified-person (to read), at the outset of the proposed work. These four factors are useful in creating an urge to read the same work, in the mind of a person.

Bhartṛhari, a famous grammarian of Samskṛt language, having a desire in mind, to write an introductory work, called Vākyapadīya, on Mahābhāṣya of Patañjali, has indicated the said factors, in detail in the first 43 verses of the work. The actual work starts from verse 44.

In the verses 24, 25, and 26, Bhartṛhari enumerates eight things as the subject of Vyākaraṇaśāstra. They are as follows–

1.	Śabda :	1.	Prakṛti and Pratyaya (root and suffix)
		2.	Pada and Vākya (word and sentence)
2.	Artha :	1.	Prakṛtipratyayārtha (meaning of root and suffix)
		2.	Padavākyārtha (meaning of word and sentence)
3.	The relation between Śabda and Artha :	1.	Kāryakāraṇabhāva (relation of cause and effect)
		2.	Yogyatā (compatibility)
4.	Purpose :	1.	Arthajñāna (knowledge of meaning)
		2.	Dharma (merit)

Of the two purposes, Dharma is important and eventually it is in the form of Mokṣa (salvation). Therefore, the very purpose of the study of Vyākaraṇaśāstra is Mokṣa. Since Brahmaprāpti (attaining Brahman) itself is Mokṣa, the Brahman has to be defined first. With this view in mind, Bhartṛhari describes the unqualified-secondless-Brahman in the first verse. Needless to say one who is interested in the above things is qualified to read this work and the relation between the purpose and the book is that between the proposed and proposer:

(Introduction to Vākyapadīya-Verses 1 to 43) Discription of Brahman

अनादिनिधनं ब्रह्म शब्दतत्त्वं यदक्षरम्।
विवर्ततेऽर्थभावेन प्रक्रिया जगतो यतः ।।

1. anādinidhanam brahma śabdatattvam yadakṣaram
vivartate' rthabhāvena prakriyā jagato yataḥ

Summary : Which Brahman, being beginningless, deathless, imperishable and the śabdatattva (noumenon of Śabda), manifests into objects and by which the universe is created .... (the first five verses are a 'kulaka' and therefore the four verses have to be construed alongwith the correlative sentence, i.e., prāptyupāyo' nukāraśca *tasya* vedaḥ-Veda is a device to attain such a Brahman, in the fifth verse).

Commentary : Both the correlatives in the verse, viz ; yat & yataḥ, indicate that this as well as the second, third and fourth verses are parts of a five-verse-kulaka. So we can get a complete meaning only after the fifth verse is construed alongwith the earlier four verses.

Here in the verse, the word 'yataḥ' is not in ablative case, but since the word is read in Ādyādigaṇa, the suffix 'tasi' is applied to the root in instrumental case and therefore the word is in instrumental case. Yataḥ-yena.

Akṣaram means that which is indestructible. Na + kṣaram-Akṣaram. The word connotes somethingelse too-aśnute (one which pervades)-one which, according to the context, pervades the meaning. It can be a word or sentence. By employing this word, i.e., Akṣāram, it is denoted by the author that word and sentence are the subject of this book. Since sentence rather than a word is important, the word 'Vākya' has got the pūrvanipāta (coming first in a Samāsa) and the work related to Vākya and Pada is Vākyapadīya.

Notes : Birth and death are inevitable to everything on earth. Even things like the Earth are there since the starting of the Yuga and they would perish at the time of Pralaya (the Delusion). Unlike these things the Brahman is eternal. It has neither Birth nor Death and that'swhy it is eternal. Such a Brahman manifests in the form of the Universe. Example-Rajjusarpa (the rope mistaken for a serpent in poor lighting). Here the rope appears like a serpent without giving up its original form. The form of a serpent is subject to illusion. Immediately after conceiving that it is a rope, the illusion of a serpent is gone (the Rajjujñāna destroys the Sarpajñāna). Similarly, as soon as one attains the

Brahmajñāna, all the illusions are gone. Brahman is the Creator of this world. Brahman itslef is the cause of the manifestation of the Universe. It means that the Brahman is the Upādānakāraṇa of the manifestation of the Universe and at the same time it is the Nimittakāraṇa of the Creation as well.

Vāk or the Speech is of four types, viz. Parā, Paśyantī, Madhyamā and Vaikhary. Among them, Parāvāk is nothing but the Cetananirguṇādvayabrahma (the conscious-unqualified-secondless Brahman), that is acceptable to Advaitavedānta school. Paśyantī, Madhyamā and Vaikhary are the manifestations of Parā. Therefore, Parāvāk, in the form of Sphoṭaśabda, is Brahman itself. This doctrine of Vaiyākaraṇas is indicated by the author through the word 'śabdatattvam'.

Intro : the author says that the Brahman, which is seen in the form of śabdatattva, is single and has got no different entities, but the same, due to different powers manifests to be many-

एकमेव यदाम्नातं भिन्नं शक्तिव्यपाश्रयात्।
अपृथक्त्वेऽपि शक्तिभ्यः पृथक्त्वेनेव वर्तते।।

2. ekameva yadāmnātam bhinnam śaktivyapāśrayāt
aprthaktvepi śaktibhyah prthaktveneva vartate

Sum : Although single, which is described in Vedas to be in so many forms, due to its having been the basis of different powers, and although not different, is seen as different from the powers inherent in itself.

Com : = In truth, the Brahman is one and only one. None of the three differences, viz. ṣajātīya, vijātīya and svagata, is applicable to that. In many a context this concept is elaborated in Upaniṣads. Such a Brahman has become the basis to Avidyā or Māyā, which has got the three guṇas, viz. Sattva, Rajas and Tamas. Māyā has got so many powers. It is due to that so many forms of Brahman are seen. This concept is elaborated in Upaniṣads. The implication is that although Brahman is only one and not different from power, it is due to the difference of powers that the same looks to be different.

Notes : The Brahman, coupled with Māyāśakti, is the cause of Creation, Existence and Destruction of the world. The same Brahman is called Saguṇa. Nirguṇabrahman cannot be the cause of the above factors. Nirguṇabrahman is nothing but Mokṣa or salvation itself.

Intro : The difference is felt due to the Kālaśakti (power of time) of Brahman- says the author-

अध्याहितकलां यस्य कालशक्तिमुपाश्रिताः
जन्मादयो विकाराः षड् भावभेदस्य योनयः ।।

3. adhyāhitakalām yasya kālaśaktimupāśritāḥ
janmādayo vikārāḥ ṣaḍ bhāvabhedasya yonayaḥ

Sum : Which, due to attribution, appears to be different and the different forms of which are caused by the six transformations, i.e., Birth etc., having based on time-power.

Com : Brahman has got a power called time. The very form of time is Kṣaṇa or second. By multiplying the seconds, we get minutes, hours, days, weeks, months, years etc., which are time-points. The same power is attributed to the Parabrahman and hence we get Birth, Existance, Change, Development, Decay and Destruction-the six transformations of Ātman (enumerated in Yāska's Nirukta). The order is due to the application of time-power to the manifestation of Brahman. Time is a manifestation of Māyā.

Notes : Here in this verse Bhāva means Parabrahman, in the form of existence. Vikāra denotes Vivarta or Manifestation. This is clarified in 36th verse of Jātisamuddesa of 3rd Kāṇḍa (Vākyapadīya.)

Intro : In this verse it is said that the generally discussed four things, viz. Jīva, Bhoktā, Bhogyam and Anubhava, are also the manifestation of Brahman–

एकस्य सर्वबीजस्य यस्यचायमनेकधा ।
भोक्तृभोक्तव्यरूपेण भोगरूपेण च स्थितिः ।।

4. ekasya sarvabījasya yasyaceyamanekadhā
bhoktṛbhoktavyarūpeṇa bhogarūpeṇa ca sthitiḥ

Sum : Which, eventhough single, is the seed (criterion) of the entire universe and has got the manifestations of the Enjoyer, the Enjoyed (thing)and Enjoyment.

Com : Enjoyer of Jīva is the reflection of Brahman due to human ignorance or Avidyā. He has got life and hence he is called Bhoktā (enjoyer). The manifestation of Brahman, which is Jaḍa (lifeless) is called Bhogya or the enjoyed. Sukha and Duḥkha (comfort and worry) are also lifeless, but since they are the reflections of 'cit', they are called Anubhava or enjoyment. So much so that due to human ignorance, Brahman appears to be the enjoyer, enjoyed and enjoyment. All this is the manifestation of Brahman.

Notes : Each and everything on earth has got some cause or the other. For example, clay is the cause of earthen pot, threads are of cloth, and gold of ornaments. Clay cannot be the cause of cloth. On the other hand Brahman is the cause of all the things. No universe other than Brahman does exist. So much so that the usage of the word 'sarvabījasya' is quite appropriate.

Intro : Having described the Brahman to be attained in four verses, the author shows the way to attain the same–

प्राप्त्युपायोऽनुकारश्च तस्य वेदो महर्षिभिः ।
एकोऽप्यनेकवर्त्मेव समाम्नातः पृथक् पृथक् ।।

5. prāptyupāyonukāraśca tasya vedo maharṣibhiḥ
ekópyanekavartmeva samāmnātaḥ pṛthak pṛthak

Sum : Veda, which is also the reflection of Brahman, is the device to attain such a Brahman. Although one, the Veda is being recited differently by sages, as if it has got so many paths.

Com : Salvation or Mokṣa is the goal of the study of Vyākaraṇa. Mokṣa means attaining Brahman, which is described in the first four verses. Veda is the only device to attain Brahman. Attaining Brahman means Brahmabhāva. The same is called Mokṣa. That Veda is a reflection of Brahman. Veda is only one. But since humanbeings in Kaliyuga have got less longevity and it is not possible to recite the entire Veda, Ṛṣis, for the sake of convenience have shown different paths like-Ṛk, Sāma, Yajur and Atharva- and Samhitá, Pada, Krama, Śikha, Mālā, Jaṭā and Ghana.

Notes : 'Upāya' is that which is taken to solve some problem and given up after completion of the task (upādāya heyaḥ-upāyaḥ). It is stated by Bhartṛhari himself in 2.38. Nageśa in his commentary (i.e. Udyota) on Mahābhāṣya (3-1-96) states that it is Sādhu (correct) by adding it to Pṛṣodarādi (Pāṇini 6-3-109).

Brahman is Sarvajña and so also Veda. Therefore, Veda is the reflection of Brahman. Anukāra means Anukṛti or Anukaraṇa, i.e. reflection.

Description of Veda (6-10)

Intro : Now the author explains the form and greatness of Veda–

भेदानां बहुमार्गत्वं कर्मण्येकत्रचाङ्गता ।
शब्दानां यतशक्तित्वं तस्य शाखासु दृश्यते ।।

6. bhedānām bahumārgatvam karmaṇyekatracāṅgatā
śabdānām yataśaktitvam tasya śākhāsu dṛśyate

Sum : It is seen that each Branch of the (four) Vedas viz. Ṛk, Yajur, Sāma and Atharvaṇa have got many paths, they are subordinate in a single ritual and the Śabdas have got a fixed capacity.

Com : A single Veda is devided into four. Among them Ṛgveda has got 21, Yajurveda 101, Sāmaveda 1000, and Atharvaveda 9 branches. This only is said to be Bahumārgatva of Śākhas.

A single Yāga might have been mentioned in many a śākhā. This does not mean that the same Yāga is differently considered. It is one and the same Yāga. While pronouncing the God-invoking-hymns, things, like ghee, are sacrificed in fire-it is called Yāga. Here, the Sacrifice is (important) principal and the hymns, the Gods invoked, and things offered in Fire are subordinate. It means that the hymns etc. are helpers in the Yāga ritual. The quality of being helpful of hymns in various branches to the same Yāga is indicated by the word 'angatvam'. So much so that a single word or sentecne or discourse may be found in different branches and in such a case that will be useful to the ritual of the same śākhā, with the same Svara (accent) and thus becomes fruitful.
Intro : The Smṛtis have got their origin in Vedas and thus also the glory of Vedas is clear-says the author–

स्मृतयो बहुरूपाश्च दृष्टादृष्टप्रयोजनाः ।
तमेवाश्रित्य लिंगेभ्यो वेदविद्भिः प्रकल्पिताः ।।

7. smṛtayo bahurūpāśca drsṭādṛṣṭa prayojanāḥ
tamevāśritya lingebhyo vedavidbhiḥ prakāśitāḥ

Sum : Smṛtis (codes) of various types with tangible and intangible objectives are formulated on the basis of the Veda, from its evidence by sages, erudite in its purport.
Com : The sages, having conceived the meaning of Veda, through their clairvoyance, have composed some codes which will reflect the meaning of Veda, for the sake of common man. They are authentic since they are originated from Vedas (the same point is elaborated by the author by 10 from verse 133). The codes are various. Some have got tangible evidence in Vedas. Others have got their origin in śiṣṭācāra or Āryan convention. They indicate objectives of both direct and indirect. The latter occur in another birth and another world.
Intro : The so called Darśanas, which are different from each other are also originated from Veda-says the author–

तस्यार्थवादरूपाणि निश्रिताः स्वविकल्पजाः ।
एकत्विनां द्वैतिनां च प्रवादा बहुधा मताः ।।

8. tasyārthavādarūpāṇi ni śritaḥ svavikalpajāḥ
ekatvinām dvaitinām ca pravādā bahudhā matāḥ.

Sum : There are different schools of Monoists and Dualists, which are started depending on their own different approaches as well as the eulogising and cencuring sentences in Vedas, called Arthavāda.
Com : Cārvāka, Bauddha, Jaina, Ārhata, Digambara, Vaiśeṣika, Nyāya, Sāmkhya, Yoga, Pūrvamīmāmsā, Uttaramīmāmsā etc. Darśanas are started -

Veda as the base. All these Darśanas are built depending on Arthavādas and other likewise sentences. Even Cāvākas or ethiests refer to Vedic sentences to substantiate their own theory. The authors of different Darśanas, at times, pick up some sentence or the other from Veda and attribute some meaning, which is sometimes quite opposite. That's why there are so many Darśanas.

Notes : In spite of the proprieties and improprieties in the interpretation the author of each Darśana proves that his views, thought and theory are perfect and at of others are imperfect.

Intro : Different Darśanas are composed by scholars, who are pragmatic in their appraoch and hence not acceptable to each other and since there is the possibility of giving a different interpretation to the Vedic sentences those reffered to - they are bound to be unauthoritative. Then the question arises - which thing is the real one? - the author answers the same–

सत्या विशुद्धिस्तत्रोक्ता विद्यैवैकपदागमा ।
युक्ता प्रणवरूपेण सर्ववेदाविरोधिना ।।

9. satyā viśuddhistatroktā vidyaivaikapadāgamā
yuktā praṇavarūpeṇa sarvavādāvirodhinā

Sum : Brahman, in the form of knowledge, which is not contradictory to any school, which has got a single goal, which is pure and real, - is said in Veda by the word 'OM' (or Praṇava). (So the same is the real thing).

Com : Veda is interpretted by many in many ways. The notions they expressed are not the very purport of Veda. On the other hand, Vedic sentences, either directly or indirectly rest in the Brahman in the form of knowledge. That is real.

Notes : Advaita Vedānta advocates the same Brahman. This school feels that the theories of all the other schools are rungs of a ladder of which the goal would be Brahman and like thus all of them are applicable to itself. The other Darśanas are different. They are built with hatred against others and undue affection in their own theories. Advaita Dar śana is not like that, rather at times it appreciates the etheist schools too.

Intro : The author says that not only Śikṣā Vyākaraṇa etc., which are famous as Vedāṅgas, but also Purāṇas are written by Vedic scholars, to bring out the knowledge lying in Vedas, for the common man–

विधातुस्तस्य लोकानामंगोपांगनिबन्धनाः ।
विद्याभेदाः प्रतायन्ते ज्ञानसंस्कारहेतवः ।।

10. vidhātustasya lokānām aṅgopāṅganibandhanāḥ
vidyābhedāḥ pratāyante jñānasamskārahetavaḥ

Sum : Different disciplines, which are sources of knowledge and culture, are developed on the divisions and sub-divisions of the Veda, which is the creator of the entire Universe.

Com : Brahman, depending on Veda has created the Universe. So Veda is the source of creation. In order to understand the Veda, Angas like Śikṣā and Upāngas like Purāṇas have come into existence. The sages have developed them.

Notes : There are six Vedāngas, viz. Śikṣā, Vyākaraṇam, Chandas, Niruktam, Jyautiṣam and Kalpam. These are called Ṣaḍangas. Purāṇam, Nyāyaḥ Mīmāṃṣā and Dharmaśāstram are called Upāngas. The knowledge of omen etc. is achieved from Vedāngas and that of Svapnavipāka (the result of dreams) as well as Karmavipāka (the result of Karma) is achieved through Upāngas. Mīmāmsā is useful for the knowledge of Ātmatattva and Dharmaśāstra for Dharmasamskāra.

Discription of Vyākaraṇa (11-22):–

Intro : Having described Veda by five verses, the author attempts to glorify Vyākaraṇa, one of the Vedāngas by three verses in order to encourage the students in its study–

आसन्नं ब्रह्मणस्तस्य तपसामुत्तमं तपः ।
प्रथमं छन्दसामंगं प्राहुर्व्याकरणं बुधाः ।।

11. āsannam brahmaṇastasya tapasāmuttamam taph
prathamam chandasāmangam prāhurvyākaraṇam budhāḥ

Sum : the sages say that Vyākaraṇa is nearest to Brahman and a means of attaining Brahman, i.e., Veda, the foremost of all spiritual training, and the most important of Vedangas.

Com : Patañjali, the author of Mahābhāṣya, has enumerated five primary purposes, viz. 1. Rak ṣā or the protection of Vedas 2. Ūhā, that is the knoweldge to replace certain word by another according to the need during rituals, 3. Āgama, the Injunction, 4. Lāghava or brevity and 5. Asamdeha or non-ambiguity. Here, in this verse Bhartṛhari elaborates the first three of them. Of the three the first two are purposes, whereas the third one is an authority in the study of Vyākaraṇa (the term is untranslatable; vy ākr-iyante apa ś ābdebhya ḥ t ṛthakkriyante iti vy ākara ṇam - it is an instrument which seperates correct Śabdas from incorrect Śabdas).

Notes : The phrase-'āsannam Brahma ṇaḥ' indicates the first two purposes, whereas the other one, i.e., 'taspasāmuttamam tapaḥ' indicates the authority of

Veda in the study of Vyākaraṇa. Vyākaraṇa is nearer to Veda. Words in Veda are both similar and disimilar to the words in secular jargoan, but with the same meaning. The difference is known only through Vyākaraṇa. here are some examples–

Secular	*Meaning*	*Vedic*
gṛhṇāmi	I'm holding	gṛbhṇāmi
śamjahāra	killed/withheld	samjabhāra
dadhāra	put on/held	dādhāra
hanti	killing	hanati
dugdhe	milking	duhre
karṇaiḥ	with ears	karṇebhiḥ

The difference in the form is known only through Vyākarana. Thus the Veda is being preserved by Vyākaraṇa.

'At dawn the sacrifice is offered to Sun, whereas at dusk the deity would be Agni (or Fire). In this Mantra we find the word 'Sūryāya' and it is useful for dawn-sacrifice. For the dusk-sacrifice we have to replace the word'Sūryāya' by 'Agnaye', since the offer is made to Agni. The said process is called 'Ūhā'. To replace a word by another with the same case-ending, one needs the help of Vyākaraṇa. Thus Vyākaraṇa is nearer to Veda.

There are many kinds of 'Tapas', like Brahmacaryam and Adhaśśayyā. (celibacy and sleeping on floor only). The result of the same would be felt only in another world (i.e., after death). The result is called Adṛṣṭaphala (the result that cannot be seen). The study of Vyākaraṇa is preferable to other Tapas as apart from Adṛṣṭa in the form of Dharma, we can have two Dṛṣṭaphalas (results that can be seen), i.e. the knowledge of correctness and knowledge of meaning of words. Veda ordains that one should study Vyākaraṇa (niṣkāraṇo Dharmaḥ, Ṣaḍaṅgo Vedo 'dhyetavyo jñeyaśca- Vedic sentence quoted by Patañjali in Paspaśāhnika of Mahābhāṣyam - Chowkhamba, Varanasi, 1987) without expectding anything in return. Vyākaraṇa is important among the Ṣaḍangas (pradhānam ca ṣa ḍaṅgeṣu Vyākaraṇam, pradh āne ca kṛto yatnaḥ phalavān bhavati; laghvartham cādhyeyam Vyākaraṇam, na cantareṇa śabd āśśakyā vijñātum- Patañjali in Paspaśāhnika of Mahābhāṣyam - Chowkhamba, Varanasi, 1987) and to know the correct Śabdas in the easiest way one has to study Vyākaraṇa-this idea is expressed by the phrase 'tapasāmuttamam tapaḥ 'and' prathamam chandasāmangam'.

Intro : The author explains the other purpose, viz. brevity, of the study of Vyākaraṇa–

प्राप्तरूपविभागाया यो वाचः परमो रसः ।
यत्तत्पुण्यतमं ज्योतिः तस्य मार्गोऽयमाजजसः ।।

12. prāptarūpavibhāgāyāḥ yo vācaḥ paramo rasaḥ
    yattatpuṇyatamam jyotiḥ tasya mārgolyamāñjasaḥ

Sum : This Vyākaraṇa is the easiest and shortest way to know the lot of correct Śabdas or Sādhuśabdas, which is the supreme essence of speech, found in so many forms like phonemes, words, sentences etc. and which is the holiest light.
Com : Both right and wrong Śabdas are employed for communication. There the lot of right Śabdas is the essence of ripe-speech, and to know that Vyākaraṇa is the only easiest way.
Intro : The fifth purpose of the study of Vyākaraṇa, viz. Asamdeha, which means understanding a Śabda without ambiguity is explained by the author–

अर्थप्रवृत्तितत्त्वानां शब्दा एव निबन्धनम् ।
तत्त्वावबोधः शब्दानां नास्ति व्याकरणादृते ।।

13. arthapravṛttitattvānām śabdā eva nibandhanam
    tattvāvabodhasśabdānām nāsti vyākaraṇādṛte

Sum : Śabdas are the sole guide to the objects. The understanding of the truth about Śabdas is not possible without Vyākaraṇa.

Com : Objects are two-fold: those conspicuous in the world and those which are in the mind of the speaker, like heaven, hell, salvation etc. To explain both the above things we need Śabdas. A Śabda can be understood only by Vyākaraṇa and by no other means and the Śabda employed with the knowledge of Vyākaraṇa would be unambiguous.

The exact form and the nourishment it needs are essential to every objeet (thing). Absence of either is called Vaikalya. The Śabda would get both from Vyākaraṇa. Without Vyākaraṇa the noumenon of Śabdas would not be concevaible and then the unambiguous meaning of the Śabda cannot be identified.
Intro : The author puts forth another purpose of Vyākaraṇa, i.e. Mokṣa (Salvation from worldly bindings)–

तद् द्वारमपवर्गस्य वाङ्. मलानां चिकित्सकम्।
पवित्रं सर्वविद्यानामधिविद्यं प्रकाशते।।

14. tad dvāramapavargasya vāṅmalānām cikitsakam
pavitram sarvavidyānāmadhividyam prakāśate

Sum : A gateway to liberation, a cure to the blemishes of speech, purifier of all (other) disciplines, it shines as being applied to them.

Com : One has to identify the root and suffix, the applications they get, the Sthāna and Prayatna of the constituent phonemes therein and use a Śabda according to the grammatical tradition. Thus he would get Dharma through which his sins will perish and he gets purity of mind through which Salvation can be attained. Āyurveda and Yogaśāstra purify phisical as well as mental blemishes respectively, whereas Vyākaraṇa purifies the blemishes of speech (i.e. incorrect Śabdas). A grammarian would never employ incorrect Śabdas, which will cause unfavourable results.

Notes : Correctness or perfection (of Śabdas) is controlled by Vyākaraṇa. The entire gamut of Arts is regulated by perfect Śabdas. Therefore, Vyākaraṇa is very much indispensable. In other words, Vyākaraṇa is respected by every other discipline. On the other hand, the author has to be ashamed of the usage of incorrect Śabdas.

Intro : Knowledge of correct and incorrect Śabdas is also another purpose of study of Vyākaraṇa, through that we attain Mokṣa - says the author–

यथार्थजातयः सर्वाः शब्दाकृतिनिबन्धनाः।
तथैव लोके विद्यानामेषा विद्या परायणम्।।

15. Yathārthajātayaḥ sarvāḥ śabdākṛtinibandhanāḥ
tathaiva loke vidyānāmeṣā vidyā parāyaṇam

Com : Just as all thing-classes depend upon Śabda-classes in the world, all the disciplines depend upon this Vyākaraṇa.

Com : All disciplines are in the form of language (Śabda). The language is analysed by Vyākaraṇa. All the worldly Śabdas need Vyākaraṇa. The same Śabdas which are there in secular texts are there in Vedas also (This point is made clear by Patañjali in Mahābhāṣya under kārake (Pāṇini 1.4.23) and by Śabaraswāmy at the onset of Bhāṣya on Jaimini's Mimāmsāsūtras). Although there are some peculiar Śabdas in Vedas, they too are analysed by Vyākaraṇa, i.e., they are also identified. Therefore, the Śabdas in Vedic literature too need Vyākaraṇa.

Notes : The Śabdas have got some meaning. The relation is that seen between cause and effect. There are the classes like Ghaṭatva and Paṭatva in the meanings. The cause of these classes is that in the Śabdas. So much so that, the class in the Śabda is the cause of the class in the Artha. Likewise, Vyākaraṇa is the cause of all the disciplines.

Intro : It is not simply because Vyākaraṇa analyses the Vedic paradigms that it is called an instrument in attaining Mokṣa, rather by directly leading to Śabdabrahman too, the Vyākaraṇa would be the threashold of Salvation-states the author–

इदमाद्यं पदस्थानं सिद्धिसोपानपर्वणाम्।
इयं सा मोक्षमाणानामजिह्मा राजपद्धतिः ।।

16. idamādyam padasthānam siddhisopānaparavaṇām
iyam sā mokṣamāṇānāmajihmā rājapaddhatiḥ

Sum : It is the first rung on the ladder towards Salvation, it is the strait royal road for those desirous of attaining Mokṣa.

Intro : It is proposed in the Upaniṣads that Ātmasamskāra through Śravaṇa, Manana and Nididhyāsana is called Mokṣa. It is so because the Avidyā perishes due to Ātmasākṣātkāra and hence the latter can be a means of attaining salvation. Then how can it be that Śabdasākṣātkāra will be an instrument for the same purpose ?– the author responds that since the Ātm ā is in the form of Śabda there won't be amiss in saying so–

अत्रातीतविपर्यासः केवलामनुपश्यति।
छन्दस्यःछन्दसां योनिमात्मा छन्दोमयीं तनूम्।।

17. atrātītaviparyāsaḥ kevalāmanupaśyati
chandasyaśchandasām yonimātmā chandomayīm tanūm

Sum : The puruṣa, who has passed beyond defects in it (i.e. in Vyākaraṇa) and is capable of protecting the Vedas observes that (Brahman) which is the source of the Vedas and the very soul (i.e. Parāvāk) of which is constituted by Vedas.

Com : One can well understand the meaning of Vedas but not before he realises the exact form of Śabda. In other words, since the meaning of a word alters by difference in the form (due to shortening/lengthening or accent), the very meaning of that particular Śabda cannot be conceived. Therefore, one who is beyond illusions and defects concerning Vyākaraṇa can only observe the perfect form of Śabda and through the same can realise the 'Parāvāk', which is nothing but the soul or Ātmā.

Intro : The author praises Vyākaraṇaśastra by five verses–

प्रत्यस्तमितभेदाया: यद्वाचो रूपमुत्तमम्।
यदस्मिन्नेव तमसि ज्योतिश्शुद्धं विवर्तते।।

18. pratyastamitabhedāyāḥ yadvāco rūpamuttamam
yadasminneva tamasi jyotisśuddham vivartate

Sum : Which (Vyākaraṇa) is the supreme essence of speech, free of any difference, which pure light appears to have taken several forms in this darkness of manifestation ....

Com : The difference of phonemes is due to the (revealing) sounds. The phonemes would amalgamate in the Parāvāk. Vyākaraṇa is a distinguished form of Parāvāk as the latter can be known only through the former.

Notes : On the other hand, Vyākaraṇa is like a lamp, which shines by itself and simultaneously illuminates the things around. Such Vyākaraṇa got united in Vaikharyvāk. Since the real form of Vyākaraṇa is not clearly seen in Vaikhary and the same is called 'darkness' or 'obscurity', the grammatical functions won't apply to Vaikharyvāk. Nor will it be a tool in the expression of meaning. So it is rightly termed 'obscurity'. Rather it reveals the Madhyamāvāk which is the subject of grammar and hence the grammarians consider the Vaikhary to have united with Vyākaraṇa 'grammar' is a loose translation of 'Vyākarana'.

वैकृतं समतिकान्ता मूर्तिव्यापारदर्शनम्।
व्यतीत्यालोकतमसी प्रकाशं यमुपासते।।

19. vaikṛtam samatikranatā mūrtivyapāradar śanam
vyatītyālokatamasī prakāśam yamupāsate

Sum : Which Sphoṭa is worshipped by those who have bypassed the difference of Vaikharydhvani due to space and time, and who have gone beyond Prākṛta and Vaikṛtadhvanis.

Com : Vaiyākaraṇas accept the Sphoṭ a śabda and the same is situated beyond both Prākṛtadhvani and Vaikṛtadhvani, i.e. it is distinct from both. The Vaikṛtadhvanis are those which are found after the Sphoṭa śabda manifested itself. They vary in accordance with space and time. Such difference is not applied in Sphoṭa śabda by Vaikyākara ṇas. Prākṛtadhvanis are that which are found before the manifestation of Sphoṭaśabda. In fact, Sphoṭaśabda is situated beyond both the Dhvanis. This would be clear in verse 77 of the same Kāṇḍa.

यत्र वाचो निमित्तानि चिह्नानीवाक्षरस्मृतेः।
शब्दपूर्वेण योगेन भासन्ते प्रतिबिम्बवत्।।

20. yatra vāco nimittāni cihnānīvakṣarasmṛteḥ
śabdapūrveṇa yogena bhāsante pratibimbavat

*Sum : I*n which Sphoṭa, the signs of Prākṛtadhvani (i.e. katva and gatva, for example), which are like the scripts, shine forth like reflections in association with Śabda antecedent to all speech.

Com : In order to recollect the phonemes, there are certain signs which are collectively called 'Script' (Lipi). Likewise to remind the Sphoṭa śabda too there are certain signs called Katva, Gatva etc.. In truth, these signs are not there in Sphoṭaśabda. But they are situated in Prākṛtadhvani, which reveals the Sphoṭa-śabda. Even then, since the difference between Sphoṭaśabda and Prākṛtadhvani is not visible, the virtues are manifested in Sphoṭa śabda. For example - the white glass (made of glass) receives the red colour of the (red) object adjacent to it and looks reddish, i.e. the virtue of another object is thus visible.

अथर्वणाम्अंगिरसां साम्नामृग्यजुषस्य च।
यस्मिन्नुच्चावचा वर्णाः पृथक्स्थितिपरिग्रहाः ।।

21. atharvaṇāmangirasām sāmnāmṛgyajuṣasya ca
yasminnuccāvacā varṇāḥ pṛthaksthitiparigrahāḥ.

Sum : In which the various letter sounds (Udātta etc.) of the four Vedas, viz. Ṛk, Yajus, Sāman and Atharvan, exist with distinct identities.

Com : We find the phonemes with different accents in all the four Vedas. In truth, the accents are not there is Sphoṭaśabda. It is single, free of any quality and is in the form of knowledge. By examination it is described that the accents are not the qualities related to Sphota.

यदेकं प्रक्रियाभेदैः बहुधा प्रविभज्यते।
तद् व्याकरणमागम्य परं ब्रह्माधिगच्छति ।।

22. yadekam prakrıayabhedaıḥ bahudhā pravibhajyate
tadvyākaraṇamāgamya parambrahmādhigamyate

Sum : Which, although only one, is devided on the basis of various analytical processes-that Supreme Brahman is attained by having recourse to Vyākaraṇa.

Com : In fact, Śabda is one and only one. It manifests as Paśyantī, Madhyamā and Vaikhary. Again the same varies as Varṇa (phoneme), Pada (word), Vākyam (sentence), Vyakti (individual), Jāti (class), Sakhaṇḍa (divisible) and Akhaṇḍa (indivisible). There too the same word is analysed in different ways by different commentators. Many a Vyākaraṇa is built by Śākalya, Śākaṭāyana, Bharadvāja, Gārgya and Pāṇini. For example, the derivation of the word Rāmaḥ is given by Pāṇini as Rāma + s, by Śākaṭāyana as Rāma + ru, by Śākalya as Rāma + ri. Likewise, Bhū + a + ti, Bhū + ati and Bhava + ti, are the derivations offered by the said Vaiyākaraḥnas, respectively, for the word Bhavati. Nevertheless, both the words, Rāmah and Bhavati, which already exist are of the same form. So much so that it can be observed eventually that all the units. i.e., phonemes, words and sentences are artifical. Therefore, the common purport of all Grammarians rests in Sphoṭa only. Such a Śabda is in the form of Brahman, which is free of any qualities.

Introduction to Vyākaraṇaśāstra.

Intro : Until now the author explained the purpose of Vyākaraṇa. Hereafter, he gives an introduction to his work in order to explain the relation of his work with Vyākaraṇaśāstra-

नित्याः शब्दार्थसम्बन्धास्तत्राम्नाता महर्षिभिः ।
सूत्राणामनुतन्त्राणां भाष्याणां च प्रणेतृभिः ।।

23. nityāḥ śabdārthasambandhāḥ tatrāmnātā maharṣibhiḥ
sūtrānamanutantrāṇām bhāṣyāṇām ca praṇetṛbhiḥ

Sum : The relationships between Śabdas and their Arthas are described many a time as eternal by the authors of Sūtras, Vārtikas and Bhāṣya of Vyākaraṇa.

Com : Pāṇini, Kātyāyana and Patañjali were of the view that the relations between Śabda and Artha is eternal and hence they constructed Sūtras, Vārtikas and Mahābhāṣya, respectively.

On the other hand, if the said relation is not eternal, speakers would change the relations (i.e. the meanings of words may be changed) at random and would coin new words as well. So that a Śabda, which is correct at present may become incorrect the other day. In that case, no śabda would have a specific form and meaning and through that the Vyākaraṇa,, which depends on usage, would also become untenable. So much so that, the protector of correctness, i.e. Vyākaraṇa, could also become uncertain and useless. Therefore, if the relations of Śabdas and Arthas are uniform and standard, so would be the Vyākaraṇa related to the same, through which the correctness of Śabdas can be achieved, which in turn would render Dharma and the same Vyākaraṇa, won't be useless.

Notes : The Mīmāmsakas also hold the same view regarding the eterntity of Śabdārthasambandha (relation between śabdas and Arthas). 'Autpattikastu śabdasyārthena sambandhaḥ....' (the relation of śabda with artha is eternal) says Jaimini (MāmāmsādarŚanam 1.1.5.5 ; Anandasram, Poona, 1930). Śabaraswāmī, the author of Bhāṣya on Jaiminisūtras as well as Kumārilabhaṭṭa, the author of Śloka-Vārtika have elaborated and substantiated the concept. In regard to Vyākaraṇa, Kātyāyana, the author of Vārtikas on Pāṇini's Aṣṭādhyāyī, clearly states thus-'siddhe Śabdārthasambandhe' (the relation between śabda and Artha is eternal)-this will explain the cryptic meaning behind the very construction of Aṣṭādhāyī. Patañjali elaborated this sentence (Mahābhāṣyam, Paspaśāhnika, Chowkhamba, Varanasi, 1987).

Intro : Having explained that, since the relation of Śabda and Artha is fixed and unchangeable, the Vyākaraṇa can be a good analyser, the author goes on to impress that the Vyākaraṇa analyses the correct Śabdas through root-suffix-structure, so that the rest are considered as incorrect. On the other hand, it is much difficult to analyse both types of Śabdas and the Vyākaraṇaśastra cannot be established on an easy way. In this context, the author exhibits the body of Vyākarana consisting of eight things (astapadārthīrūpam Vyākaraṇam) bythree verses- अपोद्धारपदार्था ये ये चार्थाः स्थितलक्षणाः ।

अन्वाख्येयाश्च ये शब्दाः ये चापि प्रतिपादकाः ।।
कार्यकारणभावेन योग्यभावेन च स्थिताः ।
धर्मे च प्रत्यये चांङ्गं सम्बन्धाः साध्वसाधुषु ।।
ते लिंगैश्च स्वशब्दैश्च शास्त्रेऽस्मिन्नुपवर्णिताः ।
स्मृत्यर्थमनुगम्यन्ते केचिदेव यथागमम ।।

24. apoddhārapadārtha ye ye cārthāḥ sthitalakṣaṇāḥ
anvākhyeyāśca ye śabdāḥ ye cāpi pratipādakāḥ

25. kāryakāraṇabhāvena yogyabhāvena ca sthitāḥ
dharme ca pratyaye cāṅgam sambhandhaḥ sādhvasādhuṣu

26. te liṅgaiśca svaśabdaiśca śāstresminnupavarṇitāḥ
smṛtyarthamanugamyante kecideva yathāgamam

Sum : In this Śāstra the following eight things are described-

1.	Śabda ;	1. { Prakṛti (root) / Pratyaya (suffix)	2. Pada (word) / Vākya (sentence)
2.	Artha :	1. Prakṛtipratyayārtha (meaning of root and suffix)	
		2. Padavākyārtha (meaning of word and sentence)	
3.	Relation : between Śabda and Artha :	1. Kāryakāraṇabhāva (relation of cause and effect)	
		2. Yogyatā (compatibility)	
4.	Purpose :	1. Arthajñāna (knowledge of meaning)	
		2. Dharma (merit)	

Com : All the said eight things are described in Vyākaraṇa, through characteristic features and through their names. Among the correct and incorrect Śabdas, only correct Śabdas are analysed, for brevity, in accordance with Śāstra.

Notes : Meaning is comprehended only through sentence, So Vaiyākaraṇas believe that only sentence is genuine. The correctness of Śabda is decided by Vyākaraṇa. Since sentences are innumerable and hence it is not possible to show the correct ones, the Vaiyākaraṇas extracted words from them. Since words are also innumerable they have separated the roots and suffixes, which like their meanings, are artificial, In Vyākaraṇa, therefore, it is the otherway round we find the order, i.e. root + suffix, word, sentence. But, in fact, the real unit is sentence and roots and suffixes are artificial, whereas the word is in between them. It is the opinion of Bhartṛhari that the meanings of roots, suffixes and words are Apoddhārapadārthas (artificially extracted meanings). As a matter of fact, one can get the meaning or cognition through both correct and incorrect Śabdas invariably. But, Dharma can be achieved only through correct Śabdas and hence the Vyākaraṇa initiated the analysis of only correct Śabdas. In this process it is understood that the rest of the Śabdas, i.e. not analysed by Vyākaraṇa, are incorrect. Even vice versa is possible, and the result is the same. But since incorrect Śabdas are more than correct Śabdas, it is neither wise nor feasible. So much so that it is due to brevity, that Vyākaraṇa analyses the correct Áabdas only. The said eight things are the subject of Vyākaraṇaśāstra. Since Vākyapadīya is a commentary on Patañjali's Mahābhāṣya, it also elaborates the concepts of eight things. That'swhy Helārāja, one of the commentators of Vākyapadīya, at the beginning of Padakāṇḍa remarks thus- 'as Vākyapadīya discusses the eight things'.

Pāṇini instituted two kinds of roots, eight kinds of suffixes and through some applications combined them to form into Śabdas (words). Through words, he achieved perfection of sentences. A break-up of the roots and suffixes is given hereunder :

1. Dhatus and 2. Prātipadikas – roots

Pratyayas – 8 types :

1. sub-suffixes (su, au, jas etc.) – 21
2. Strīpratyayas – 9
3. Taddhitapratyayas – 200 odd
4. Sanādipratyayas – 12
5. Vikaraṇapratyayas – 22
6. Lakāras – 10

7. Tiṅ-pratyayas – 18
8. Kṛt-pratyayas – 110

Pāṇini attributed (artificial) meaning to the roots as well as the Pratyayas on his own. So the meanings of both the things are not natural.

In Vyākaraṇa, word is exhibited as more a real thing than root and suffix and sentence as more real than word. So word is there in between. According to Patañjali, roots and suffixes are extracted from words and the latter from a sentence. The same process, which is rather artificial is termed by Bhartṛhari as Apoddhāra. Artificial creation of parts from Akhaṇḍavākya (indivisible sentence) is called Apoddhāra.

In Apoddhāra-process, Śabdas in the form of roots and suffixes, with meanings are accepted and through them the sentences, which are real, are known with their meanings.

In the verse 24, the word 'Apoddhārapadārthāḥ' denotes two things-meanings of root and suffix, 'sthitalakṣaṇāḥ' denotes the meanings of word and sentence, 'Anvākhyeyāḥ, denotes word and sentence and 'Pratipādakāḥ' stands for root and suffix. Thus four things are suggested by this verse.

Patañjali explains that there are two types of relations between Śabdas and Arthas : 1. Kāryakāraṇabhāva (the relation of cause and effect) and 2. Yogyatā (compatibility). Initially, the meaning comes to the mind of the speaker. If he had a desire to express (vivakṣā) the same then the appropriate Śabda comes to his mind. So much so that by the process it is clear that meaning is the cause and Śabda is the effect, and the relation of cause and effect exists between them. One the other hand, as soon as the speaker employes the Śabda, the listner gets the meaning. In this process quite opposite is the case, i.e. Śabda is the cause and Artha is the effect. Like thus the relation of cause and effect between Śabda and Artha is established. The sense-organs are naturally capable of receiving things and in the same manner, Śabdas are naturally capable enough to render meanings. (Sambandhasamuddeśa-Padakāṇḍa-verse-29). Tādātmya (synthesis with each other) is Yogyatā, that Śabda and Artha posses. The same is the relation. Such a relation has no beginning, nor is it artificial.

The purpose of Vyākaraṇa is claimed to be two-fold : Arthajñāna (cognition of meaning) and Dharma (a virtue useful in attaining Mokṣa-salvation). The latter is, in truth, of two types-Pravṛtti and Nivṛtti. The former is useful in attaining comforts in this world whereas the latter is for Moksā. Two kinds of relations and two types of purposes are proposed in verse 25.

The Vyākaraṇaśāstra analyses the said eight things. The same things are expounded in this treatise. Brahmakāṇḍa deals with both the purposes, i.e. Arthajñāna and Dharma. Vākyakāṇḍa discusses the sentence and its meaning. Prakṛti, Pratyaya, their meanings, the relation of cause and effect and capability-are the subject matter of Padakāṇḍa. In the first Kāṇḍa, the capacity of Śabda in rendering meaning is explained from verse 44 onwards. Similarly, in verse 93, it is said that the Jāti, intrinsic in a śabda is the cause of expression of meaning. Verse 27 deals with the result of Dharma (Sādhavo dharmasādhanam). In verse 140 prosperity is stated to be the result of Dharma. Mokṣa (salvation) is explained in verses-14, 16, 22, and 132.

In Vyākaraṇa, suffixes like-tavya, anīyay, ti etc. and roots like-bhū, edh, kanyā, janapada etc. are exhibited. Some words like tvā, mā, vām, nau, vaḥ, te, me and sentences like-eikāgārikaḥ (a thief who seeks an isolated house), śrotriyaḥ (one who recites Veda), Hare'va (O!Vi ṣ ṇu!save me) etc. are cited as examples of correct usage.

The words and sentences are supplied by Vyākaraṇa through the signs of roots and suffixes. This is denoted by the phrase 'te liṅgaiśca svaśabdaiśca' in the above verse.

Among the enumerated eight things, the conception of meaning and Dharma are exhibited as results and the rest as instruments of the results.

These three verses have given a gist of the views of Kātyāyana and Patañjali, expressed at the outset of Mahābhāṣya.

Bhartṛhari has indicated the relation of Vākyapadīya with the VyākaraṇaŚāstra, constructed by Pāṇini, Kātyāyana and Patañjali, through the verse-'nityāh śabdārthasambandhāḥ.....'

Intro : In verse 26 it is held that from among the correct and incorrect Śabdas, the correct ones are analysed by Vyākaraṇa. But how to distinguish between correct and incorrect Śabdas ? Moreover, the roots and suffixes may be useful in producing cognition, but not Dharma ? -the author answers the question-

शिष्टेभ्य आगमात्सिद्धा साधवो धर्मसाधनम् ।
अर्थप्रत्यायनाभेदे विपरीतास्त्वसाधवः ।।

27. śiṣṭebhya āgamātsiddhāḥ sādhavo dharmasādhanam
arthapratyāyanābhede viparītāstvasādhavaḥ

Sum : Eventhough there won't be any difference in explanation of meaning, only those forms, which are established by Vyākaraṇaśāstra and pronounced by śiṣṭas, are valid as instruments of Dharma and the opposite ones are incorrect (hence we cannot attain Dharma through them).

Com : Then there may be a doubt as to how to distinguish between correct and incorrect Śabdas, when both render the same meaning. For this purpose, our ancesters have set up certain standard-the śiṣṭas are those who realised the philosophy of Śabda, through transcendental capabilities. They constructed the Śāstras. Those Śabdas formed through grammatical process are correct and those which are far from such process are incorrect. The correct śabdas are instrumental in attaining Dharma, whereas the others are not. The incorrect śabdas may even generate Adharma.

Intro : Among the founders of śāstras there are two schools -Śabdas are not produced, they are eternal like atoms, are made clear by the touch of air at different organs.-this is the opinion of the first school. Śabdas are born by the touch of air at different organs. They can't be eternal like the sounds produced by the contact of drum and drumsticks-this is the contention of the second school. In ths background, according to the former school it is possible, since Śabdas are eternal, to establish that so and so Śabdas are correct and so and so are not. But how is it possible in the case of the second school, who argue that the Śabdas are produced, to establish any procedure. It's also possible in the latter school's case that fresh Śabdas can be created, a Vyākaraṇa can be written for the same and it can also be claimed that they are correct. So that the question is how to exhibit or find out an established system ? -the author answers-

नित्यत्वे कृतकत्वे वा तेषामादिर्न विद्यते।
प्राणिनामिव सा चैषा व्यवस्थानित्यतोच्यते।।

28. nityatve kṛtaktve vā teṣāmādirna vidyate
prāṇināmiva sā caiṣā vyavasthānityatocyate

Sum : Whether Śabdas are eternal or (artificial) created, they have no beginning. Their eternity is like that of the living beings (or Pravāhanityatā-eternity of a stream of water).

Com : Śabdas are eternal like living beings and they are imperishable-this is the contention of Vaiyākaraṇas. The construction of Vyākaraṇa system is justifiable only in accordance with this school and such a system won't go waste (the same answer is offered in verse 23).

On the other hand some systems are of the view that Śabdas are produced and perish like human bodies. So, since Śabdas are not eternal, according to these systems Vyākaraṇa would go to waste. But, Bhartṛhari declares, that Śabdas are eternal even in that case. It can be explained thus -Śabdas may be produced and may perish. But they are there in uninturrupted currency. They look like a stream and therefore they also can be treated as eternal. In this manner Śabdas get eternity. The same is called Pravāhanityatā and Vyavahāranityatā (stream-like-eternity and eternity due to currency).

Notes : Vaiyākaraṇas hold that Śabdas are anvil-eternals (kūṭastha-nitya) i.e. the Śabdas have an eternal form, without birth or death. Even according to other systems Śabdas could be eternal like streams. So that for them also Vyākaraṇa is not useless.

Intro : If the correctness is inherited through beginning-less-noble-tradition (or Anādisiddhaśiṣṭaparamparā) then there is no need to construct Vyākaraṇa, as the knowledge of correctness of Śabdas could be achieved through other means-the author answers the question-

नानर्थिकामिमां कश्चिद् व्यवस्था कर्तुमर्हति।
तस्मान्निबध्यते शिष्टैः साधुत्वविषया मतिः ।।

29. nānarthikāmimām kaścidvyavasthām kartumarhati
tasmānnibadhyate śiṣṭaih sādhutvaviṣayā smṛtiḥ

Sum : Nobody, without the help of Vyākaraṇa, can formulate such a pattern, which is difficult to understand and study. Therefore, the śistas, like Pāṇini, have made up this Vyākaraṇa Smṛti related to the correctness of Śabdas.

Com : The correct Śabdas can be known through noble tradition. Therefore the Vyākaraṇa is useless-is the question-but how to pronounce accents like udātta etc. ? What are the regulations of accents ? How might be the regulations of short, long etc. Vowels ? -these things, however wise he may be, one cannot explain to others without the help of Vyākaraṇa. With this view śiṣṭas have consctructed Vyākaraṇa.

Intro : Dharma can be achieved through the usage of correct Śabdas. But to standardize such correct Śabdas there is no need of Vyākaraṇa. Logic can as well be helpful. This Śabda, 'gauḥ' is correct (major premise), as it is used by śiṣtas (noblemen of Āryāvarta). *Therefore, there is no need of Vyākaraṇa-the author answers this question by five verses-*

न चागमादृते धर्मस्तर्केण व्यवतिष्ठते।
ऋषीणामपि यज्ज्ञानं तदप्यागमपूर्वकम्।।

30. nacāgamādrte dharmastarkeṇa vyavatiṣṭhate
ṛṣīṇāmapi yajjñānam tadapyāgamapūrvakam

Sum : The Dharma, cannot be established without (reasoning) Logic. Even the knowledge possessed by Ṛṣis has got the logical background.

Com : The rationalism or Hetuvāda decides everything depending on perception or Pratyakṣa. Dharma or Adharma are transcendental and since they are called 'adṛṣṭas'. The same cannot be decided by rationalism. When it is said that usage of correct Śabdas would render Dharma, such correctness has to be achieved through Vyākaraṇa and not rationalism. It also should not be questioned that depending on the inference-this Śabda is correct, since it is used by noble men, like the Śabda 'gauḥ', which is akin to the one-the hill is fiery, as it has smoke, like a kitchen-the correctness of śabdas is achieved, and therefore no seperate device like Vyākaraṇa is needed-

The Sages, having chastity, etc., studied Vedas, and performed the rites enjoined by them, in accordance with śāstras. Through such performance, they achieved the knowledge useful in getting the things of transcendental nature. In this manner their knowledge has got its roots in Vedas. They built the scriptures and systems with the help of the same knowledge and never on their own or through the means of inference. So much so that the rationalism alone cannot be the deciding factor of Dharma.

Intro : It is not legimate to say that Dharma is originated in Āgamas (Scriptures). There are a number of Scriptures, which preach customes that are useful to deceive people. For example-take the sentence-'na kāñścana pariharet' (no woman, who approached with sexual desire should be refused). Likewise, consumption of arrack is seen in Vāmācāra. In this context, how the Scripture can be an establishing factor of Dharma ?

Moreover, rationalism (or Tarka) can be helpful as far as possible. The skull of a human being is pure, since it is the limb of a being-such a logic may also be instrumental in establishing Dharma-the author answers these questions-

धर्मस्यचाव्यवच्छिन्नाः पन्थानो ये व्यवस्थिताः ।
न तान् लोकप्रसिद्धत्वात कश्चित्तर्केण बाधते ।।

31. dharmasyacāvyavacchinnāḥ panthāno ye vyavasthitaḥ
na tān lokaprasiddhatvāt kaścittarkeṇa bādhate

Sum : Which Āgamas are, devices of attaining Dharma (righteousness), established, unbroken by tradition as they are practised by śiṣṭas and since being famous, cannot be refuted by logic.

Com : There may be different Scriptures in the world. But, the Scriptures, which are meant for the prosperity of people, which are popular among śiṣṭas and which are not hated by all should not be refuted simply by applying the dry logic. The Scriptures which preach Vāmācāra are not accepted by śiṣṭas. So they cannot be factors of establishing Dharma. All the Scriptures cannot be likened to such Scriptures and refuted.

Intro : The rationalism is applied depending on the powers and their association in mundane things. In mundane things itself there are powers different from each other, i.e. all are not alike. In such a situation, the Logic cannot be applicable even in mundane things. Then how is it possible that Logic can be a deciding factor of Dharma, which is spiritualistic by nature ?-the author argues-

अवस्थादेशकालाना भेदाद् भिन्नषु शक्तिषु।
भावानामनुमानेन प्रसिद्धिरतिदुर्लभा।।

32. avasthādeśakālānam bhedādbhinneṣu śaktiṣu
bhāvānāmanumānena prasiddhiratidurlabhā

Sum : The natures of substances are very difficult to decide by inference since the properties vary due to state, place and time.

Com : A man is not strong during infancy. He is strong during the course of youth. Green pepper causes phlem. The same, if dried, kills phlem, gout and bilious nature (kapha, vāta and pitta). Water at icy mountains is cool and warm in tropical places. The water of a well, the shadow of a banian tree, a young lady and a house built of bricks-are warm in winter and cool in summer. So, the Logic is not useful in regard with Dharma, which is of transcendental nature. Only Scriptures can do the job.

Intro : It is stated in the last verse that the powers of substances change due to form, place and time. Now the author says that due to the contact with other substances too, the powers change-

निर्ज्ञातशक्तेर्द्रव्यस्य तां तामर्थक्रियां प्रति।
विशिष्टद्रव्यसंबन्धे सा शक्तिः प्रतिबध्यते।।

33. nirjñātaśakterdravyasya tāmtāmarthakriyām prati
viśiṣṭadravyasambandhe sā śaktiḥ pratibadhyate

Sum : The well-known power of a substance towards a particular activity is obstructed, when it comes in contact with another specific object.

Com : Every thing (or substance), it is obvious, has got some power to effect certain action. For example-fire has the power of burning. But when the same comes in contact with moon-stone, which is of different kind (Jāti), it looses its burning (power) capacity. So that it is not wise to decide the power and apply Logic, immediately after noticing a substance. Therefore, only Scriptures can become the very proof in regard to Dharma and Adharma, which are of transcendental nature.

Intro : The Logic offered by the most genious person can be impeccable. It will be useful in establishing Dharma and Adharma. Then there is no need of Scripture for the same purpose-the author answers the question-

यत्नेनानुमितोऽप्यर्थः कुशलैरनुमातृभिः ।
अभियुक्ततरैरन्यैरन्यथैवोपपद्यते ।।

34. yatnenānumito' pyarthaḥ, kuśalairanumātṛbhiḥ
abhiyuktatarairanyairanyathaivopapadyate

Sum : A conclusion inferred after great consideration even by logicians, with considerable scholarship, is decided otherwise by others more qualified.

Com : It should not be argued that the logic offered by a person can be stable and hence the Scripture is useless. Because, in case the logic is based on intelligence, instead of Scriptures, then a more intelligent fellow can apply the same logic to a quite opposite thing, since there is no limit to intelligence. Therefore, unestablished logic cannot decide Dharma and Adharma.

Intro : The author says that another means of knowledge, called *Abhyāsa (intuition or instinct) has to be accepted-*

परेषामसमाख्येयम् अभ्यासादेव जायते ।
मणिरूप्यादिविज्ञानं तद्विदां नानुमानिकम् ।।

35. pareṣāmasamakhyeyam abhyāsādeva jāyate
maṇirūpyādivijñānam tadvidām nānumānikam

Sum : The knowledge, like distinguishing between different diamonds, coins etc., which cannot be described for others-arises in those who possess it, only from practice, it is not inferential.

Com : Gems, Silver, Gold etc. are examined several times and their merits and demerits are decided by businessmen. Similarly, some musicians can easily identify the notes (svaras), such as Ṣadja, Gāndhāra etc.. But they cannot define the merits and demerits, they understood. The cognition they achieved is not through the famous means of cognition, i.e. Perception, Inference and Scripture. It is through Intuition. Therefore, Intuition (or Abhyāsa) has to be accepted as a means of cognition.

Notes : Dharma may not be perceivable. It is the subject of cognition of Sages, which is akin to the knowledge of gems.

Intro : The author believes that another means of congnition, i.e. *Adṛṣṭa (Fortune), has to be accepted* (apart from the six, including Abhyāsa)-

प्रत्यक्षमनुमानं च व्यतिक्रम्य व्यवस्थिताः ।
पितृरक्षःपिशाचानां कर्मजा एव सिद्धयः ।।

36. pratyakṣamanumānam ca vyatikramya vyavasthit āḥ
pitṛrakṣaḥpiśācānām karmajā eva siddhayaḥ

Sum : The Supernatural powers of departed Souls, Rākṣasas, and demons are the results of their actions in previous births. Those powers do not fall within the jurisdiction of Perception or Inference.

Com : The things faraway by place and time cannot be perceived. Wall, tree etc. may also obstruct the perception. On the other hand, fore fathers (their spirits), demons and ghosts can perceive things existing anywhere. The cause of such capability is the Karma (nemesis). They have nothing to do with the means of cognition. The power emerged through their Karma. The Karma itself is fortune. Therefore, fortune or Adṛṣṭa has to be accepted as a means of cognition.

Notes : Even the Sages have achieved the knowledge useful in identifying the Dharma through some fortune born by aceticism and not by perception etc.

Intro : The author proves that there is a means of cognition called Fortune or Adrsta-

आविर्भूतप्रकाशानाम् अनुपप्लुतचेतसाम् ।
अतीतानागतज्ञानम प्रत्यक्षान्न विशिष्यते ।।

37. āvirbhūtaprakāśānām anupaplutacetasām
atātīnāgatajñānam pratyakṣānna viśiṣyate

Sum : The knowledge of past and future, possessed by sages, whose minds are not polluted by Rajas or Tamas, and hence who are enlightened, is not different than the perceptual knowledge.

Com : The Yogin, through destruction of Rajas and Tamas, developes Sattva (all the three are Qualities). Thus they gain the knowledge useful to identify things of transcendental nature. With the help of such knowledge, they can discern past and future. Their knowledge is akin to that we get through perception. We get the perceptive cognition by the contact of sense-organs with objects. There we get a definite cognition beyond doubt. The cognition of sages is also definite and not doubtful. They discern the entire universe as we see our face in a mirror. This is due to some kind of Fortune.

Intro : The perception, which is not related to sense-organs is called illusion. Therefore, why not the perception gained by Sages be brought under this category ? śuktirajatajñāna and Rajusarpajñāna (the cognition gained through-the mistaken identity of pearl for silver and rope for serpent- which are illusions) also fall under the same category. Depending on the similarity, the cognition of Sages can be termed an illusion. Moreover, *it is against to Inference- the author answers the question-*

अतीन्द्रियानसंवेद्यान् पश्यन्त्यार्षेण चक्षुषा ।
ये भावान , वचनं तेषां नानुमानेन बाध्यते ।।

38. atīndriyānasamvedyān paśyantyārṣeṇa cakṣuṣā
ye bhāvān, vacanam teṣām nānumānena bādhyate

Sum : The word of (Sages) those who can discern the super-sensual and non-cognisable objects cannot be refuted by inferential reasoning.

Com : The things not perceivable to the human eye are visible to Yogins. They can discern the all-powerful and internal Paramātmā, the atoms which are the origin of the entire universe, the Action of atoms, Gods, the body held by Jeevatmā during the course of his transit from the physical body and the Samskāra of Karma, which render the result at a different time. They cannot be perceived by sense-organs like an image, nor can they be felt by mind like comfort and worry. Therefore, how can it be possible to compare their knowledge with Śuktirajatajñāna etc. depending upon feeble rationalism ? Inference may be defeated.

Intro : The knowledge of Sages may not be affected by inference. But the followers of their words would be affected since they do not possess much knowledge related to Sages. So much so that due to the influence of inference, some doubt or the other arises. So *one cannot decide between Dharma and Adharma and cannot act*-the author clarifies the doubt-

यो यस्य स्वमिव ज्ञानं दर्शनं नातिशंकते।
स्थितं प्रत्यक्षपक्षे तं कथमन्यो निवर्तयेत्।।

39. yo yasya svamiva jñānam darśanam nātiśankate
sthitam pratyakṣapakṣe tam kathamanyo nivartayet ?

Sum : When a man does not doubt the knowledge attained from a Yogin, as if it were his own, and stands on the side of perception, how can another make him change his mind ?

Com : Inference may not affect the knowledge of Sages. But Logic may affect followers of their words, as they do not possess the knowledge as much as the Sages do-this approach is not legitimate. The śāstra is that given by śiṣṭas. They won't say a thing which does not fall in line with śāstra. Therefore, Logic cannot restrict one, who believes that the words of śiṣṭas are a means of cognition. He, having believed their words, keeps on performing auspicious rites.

Man does not doubt a thing which is being perceived as well as the words of śiṣṭas. He considers the words on a par with perception. He trusts words like-'stones are floating on water', without doubt if they are uttered by śiṣṭas. Such a confidence he puts in their words. A Logician cannot restrict such a person from performing Dharma.

Intro : The word of a noble man is more trustworthy than the Scriptures, i.e. Vedas and Smṛtis. Even without Śrutis and Smṛtis, *the people follow, a nobleman's words* -says the author-

इद पुण्यमिदं पापम् इत्येतस्मिन् पदद्वये।
आचण्डालं मनुष्याणाम अल्पं शास्त्रप्रयोजनम्।।

40. idam puṇyamidam pāpam ityetasmin padadvaye
ācaṇḍālam manuṣyāṇām alpam śāstraprayojanam

Sum : The śāstra is of little use to people down to Candāla in judging as to which is 'puṇya' (virtue) and which is 'pāpa' (sin).

Com : In truth, Puṇya and Pāpa can be known only through Vedas. But those who did not study Vedas also know both of them through nobleman's words. One would get Puṇya by performing an auspicious action and Pāpam by the performance of inauspicious action-this fact is known to everybody. Scripture is not needed for this purpose. When someone tells about Dharma and Adharma, which are inherited from honest/noble men (āptas), to the people they trust them. Therefore, āptopadeśa (or the words of a noble/honest man) are more authentic than Vedas and Smṛtis or the so called Scriptures. People, even when the Vedas and Smṛtis do not exist, trust the words of a noble man and follow the same. Then there is no room for the doubt as to whether the śāstra is authoritative or not.

Intro : Thus, having established the authority of Scriptures, the author explains as to *following which Scripture the system of Vyākaraṇa* has come into existence-

चैतन्यमिव यश्चायमविच्छेदेन वर्तते।
आगमस्तमुपासीनः हेतुवादैर्न बाध्यते।।

41. caitanyamiva yaścāyamavicchedena vartate
āgamastamupāsīnaḥ hetuvādairna bādhyate

Sum : He, who has got the knowledge of scriptures, which shines continuously like consciousness is not disturbed by the inferential arguments of Logicians.

Com : Āgama means Śabda. It's a proof (means of cognition) stronger than Inference. He, who trusts Āgama won't surrender to the dry logical arguments. Śabda, like 'Caitanya' (consiciousness) is allpervading without interruption.

Notes : The founders and propegators of various systems have emphasized that Śabdas and Arthas denoted by them are perennial and the same can be attained by the study of Vyākaraṇa. For the same purpose, so much labour is not needed and they can be known through day to day life-one may argue on these lines of dry-logic. But the argument cannot be sustained- Śabda says that the relations between Śabda and Artha are to be known only through the study of śāstra. Rationalism or Logic goes only to some extent, not everywhere. On the ther hand, Śabda, like consciousness, exists in all beings.

Śiṣṭas have embraced the Scriptures. Even Bauddhas have accepted truth and non-violence taking Śabda (Veda) as authority and the Greek have paid attention to the condition regarding edibles and non-edibles. This is to prove, that those who do not accept the authority of Veda and Jurisprudence, follow the Śabda.

Intro : Having thus proved that Scripture is more powerful than Logic, the author now clarifies that the one, who, having neglected the Scriptures, follows the sole Logical path as a base in regard with Dharma and Adharma would certainly be vulnerable to dangers –

हस्तस्पर्शादिवान्धेन विषमे पथि धावता ।
अनुमानप्रधानेन विनिपातो न दुर्लभः ।।

42. hastasparśādivāndhena viṣame pathi dhāvatā
anumānapradhānena vinipāto na durlabhaḥ

Sum : It is not difficult to fall for him, who, like a blindman running on a rough path, with knowledge obtained from feeling of his hand, solely depends upon inferential knowledge.

Com : The Logician perceives certain thing through sense-organs and presumes another related thing which is not perceivable. He offers a similar thing as proof. If it is alright, he applies the same proof elsewhere too.

In fact, it is not legitimate to judge that due to similarity, the same is the case everywhere. That will not be sufficient to decide a thing (Viṣaya). A blindman cannot walk, even on a plain surface without help. Then how can he walk on a rough surface, like a hilly area ? On the contrary, if he, by the touch of his hand, feels that the path is even and sets foot and then infering that the entire path, due to similarity, is even starts running, he would meet with an accident. In case a man with sight helps him, nothing like that happens. In the same manner, he who without minding Vedas and Śāstras, decides Dharma and Adharma solely depending on Logic would go to Hell.

So, having taken Vedas and Śāstras as an authority, if one follows the Logic, which is not in contradiction with the former, he would know the real Dharma and Adharma.

Intro : Through the last twelve verses, the author has proved that Dharma and Adharma are decided not by Logic but by Scriptures. In this verse he concludes that *Scripture is the only instrument* in deciding Dharma and Adharma –

तस्मादकृतकं शास्त्रम् स्मृतिं च सनिबन्धनाम् ।
आश्रित्यारभ्यते शिष्टैः शब्दानामनुशासनम् ।।

43. tasmādakṛtakam śāstram smṛtim ca sanibandhanam
āśrityārabhyate śiṣṭaiḥ śabdānāmanuśāsanam

Sum : Therefore, based on the Scripture of impersonal origin and the tradition of the precept-books with their binding precepts, the Śbdānuśāsana is being started by Śiṣṭas.

Com : Logic cannot render the knowledge of correct Śabdas. The same which is the cause of Dharma, is possible only through Vyākaraṇa. Such a system is handed over sympathetically by Sages like Pāṇini, following Vedas and the Scriptures, inherited from Śiṣṭas.

Notes : The fourteen Śivasūtras, 'aiuṇ' etc. are as good as Vedic sentences and Pāṇinīyam is constructed depending upon Pratyāhāras like aṇ, ik, yaṇ etc. made out of the same Sūtras. A discussion in Atharvaveda reads thus – 'What is a Dhātu ? What is a Prātipadika ? What is a Pratyaya ?' Pāṇini borrowed terms like Dhātu, Prātipadika, Pratyaya etc. from the above source and built the treatise called Aṣṭādhyāyī for the people.

Earlier Vaiyākaraṇas like Āpiśali, Śākaṭāyana, Śākalya, Bharadvāja, Gārgya, Senaka, Gālava etc. have constructed Vyākaraṇa treatises during the course of their life. Having examined all works of earlier Vaiyākaraṇas, Pāṇini taught this Aṣṭādhyāyī.

Intro : Having explained the subject, purpose, relation and the qualified person (Anubandhacatuṣṭaya), the author begins the very *Śāstra* with this verse –

द्वावुपादानशब्देषु शब्दौ शब्दविदो विदुः ।
एको निमित्तं शब्दानाम् अपरोऽर्थे प्रयुज्यते ।।

44. dvāvupādānaśabdeṣu śabdau śabdavido viduḥ
eko nimittam śabdānām aparo'rthe prayujyate

Sum : The Vaiyākaraṇas consider that there are two types of Śabdas in functional words, one (Vaikhary) is the cause (which enlightens) of the other Śabda (Sphota)

Com : There are two types of Śabdas in Rāma, Kṛṣṇa etc., which are employed to transform some meaning or the other – 1. Vaikhary 2. Madhyamā. Vaikaryśabda is that sound produced by the movement of the parts of body like tongue, teeth, lips etc. It is audible and non-eternal. Madhyamāsśabda is that which is there in the mind. It is not produced and therefore eternal. The same is called Sphoṭaśabda. This cannot be heard by others. The Sages have established that both these Śabdas are the subject of Vyākaraṇaśāstra.

Notes : A lamp illuminates the things in darkness. Similarly, Vaikhary illuminates the Madhyamāśabda, which is there in the mind. Such an illuminated Sphoṭaśabda, which exists in the form of Madhyamāvāk, renders the meaning. Vaikhary is illuminator whereas Madhyamā is illuminated. Both are also referred to as Vyañjaka (suggestive) and Vyaṅgya (suggested), respectively. Vaikhary is the clarifying agent and Madhyamā is the clarified.

Quite different sounds are produced while the river flows rapidly, one blows a flute or drum and the birds and animals cry. These are mere sounds, and not phonemes. Such sounds are not the subject of Vyākaraṇa, as they are not the Śabdas which can express meaning. Keeping this idea in mind the author employed the word 'upādānaśabdeṣu'.

Upādāna means the most important cause. That is the Śabdas through which some meaning can be expressed to the hearer. So it (Vyākaraṇa) is about the Śabdas, which are the very cause in expression.

Intro : Some Vaiyākaraṇas, the author says, have differentiated between the suggestive (Vaikhary) and suggested (Madhyamā) Śabdas. Others view both as one and the same and say that *due to appraoch the difference is felt –*

आत्मभेदस्तयोः केचिदस्तीत्याहुः पुराणगाः ।
बुद्धिभेदादभिन्नस्य भेदमेके प्रचक्षते ।।

45. ātmabhedastayoḥ kecidastītyāhuḥ purāṇagāḥ
buddhibhedādabhinnasya bhedameke pracakṣate

Sum : Some, who follow the old theory consider that there is difference between the forms of Śabdas. Others are of the view that both the Śabdas are one and the same, but due to approach, the difference is felt (i.e. that both Kārya and Kāraṇa are different according to some and others argue that both are one and the same).

Com : Since it is suggestive, the Vaikharyśabda is the cause and since it is suggested the Madhyamā is the effect. Therefore, some argue, as it is natural that cause and effect are different from each other, both the Śabdas are different. Some others believe that effect is not at all different from cause. Since, according to the latter, there is no difference, both the Śabdas are considered to be one and the same (Abheda). On the otherhand, due to the difference in approach (Buddhi), both the Śabdas are treated to be different from each other. In other words, as Vaikharyśabda is the subject of the ear and Madhyamāśabda is the subject of the mind, both seem to be different. Strictly speakng, the Vaikharyśabda is the subject of the mind of the speaker, whereas the Madhyamāśabda is the subject of the mind of the hearer. Nevertheless, the so called difference between both the Śabdas is artificial and not natural.

To sum up, according to the formers' view the difference between both the Śabdas is natural, whereas in the latter's view it is artificial.
Intro : It sounds in 44 th verse that Madhyamāśabda is the cause of Vaikhary. *How can it be possible when the vaikhary is produced first ?* – the author answers the question –

अरणिस्थं यथा ज्योतिः प्रकाशान्तरकारणम्।
तद्वच्छब्दोऽपि बुद्धिस्थः श्रुतीनां कारणं पृथक्।।

46. araṇistham yathā jyotiḥ prakāśāntarakāraṇam
tadvacchabdo 'pi buddhisthaḥ śṛtīnām kāraṇam pṛthak

Sum : Just as the light, which is in the firestick or Araṇi (a dry piece of wood of Śamī) acts as the cause of further light, the Śabda in the mind is the cause of speech sounds.
Com : Fire, attained through charming of two pieces of dry wood (Śamī and Aśwattha) is used in the performance of Vedic rites like sacrifice. The Śamī wood in which a hole is made is called Araṇi. When the dry wood of Aśwattha is placed in the hole of Araṇi and is rotated with the help of a rope, (after some time) fire emanates from the Araṇi due to friction. Such a fire is considered to be pure for Vedic rites.

There is fire in minute form in Araṇi. Its characteristics such as shining, conduction etc. are not visible to us. But when the Araṇi is churned, the fire emanates and its characteristics are visible. Therefore people understand that the fire which is there in the Araṇi in minute form is the illuminating factor whereas the fire in magnified form is the illuminated and the former is the cause of the latter.

Similarly, the Madhyamā-śabda is there in the mind in minute form. The same having revealed, depending on the expression of the speaker and with the help of the effort one makes with the speech-organs, illuminates the Vaikhary - Śabda. That'swhy the Vaikhary Śabda is uttered in accordance with the meaning one desires to express. In other words if one wishes to express the meaning of Ghaṭa (a pot) the phonemes i.e. gh-a-ṭ-a, are uttered, which can convey the meaning. They are in that form because they are produced depending on the Sphoṭa-Śabda, which is there in minute form in the mind. On the other hand, the Vakhary sounds cannot be in that form. So much so that, the Vaikhary- Śabda is produced following the Śabda in mind and therefore both of them have got the relation of effect and cause, which is seen here in the form of illuminated and illuminator.
Intro : While substantiating his argument offered in the earlier verse that the Sphoṭaśabda is there in the mind in minute form and is suggested by the

Vaikharyśabda which is in magnified form, the author answers the following question-when Sphoṭaśabda is only one then *how come the meaning of the Śabda-cloth, is not rendered by the Vaikhary sounds of the Śabda-pot –*

वितर्कितः पुरा बुद्ध्या क्वचिदर्थे निवेशितः ।
करणेभ्यो विवृत्तेन ध्वनिना सोऽनुगृह्यते ।।

47. vitarkitaḥ purā buddhyā kvacidarthe niveśitaḥ
karaṇebhyo vivṛttena dhvaninā so 'nugṛhyate

Sum : Before pronunciation, the Śabda is distinguished (and seperated from other words), then fixed in a meaning and through the instrumentality of speech sounds, produced through the means, is expressed.

Com : Two questions arise – earlier to utterance where was the Śabda ? In what form it was ? The Sphoṭaśabda in the form of Madhyamā, which can render the meaning is there in the mind. The meaning has got amalgamated with Śabda (tādātmya of Artha with Śabda). Since Śabda and Artha are there in the same place, i.e. mind, they get mutual superimposition (Parasparādhyāsa). In other words, the Artha is superimposed on Śabda and vice-versa. Each Śabda expressing certain meaning and identified by the same meaning (Tādātmya-sambandha) is distinguished from other Śabdas in the mind by intelligence. Then the Buddhi (intelligence) enters such a Śabda in the intended meaning. This is the arrangement of Śabda and Artha in the mind before utterance.

Consequently, the speaker produces the speech-sounds, called Vaikharyśabdas, through speech-organs. The uttered Śabda becomes clear following such Vaikharydhvanis. Therefore, the Śabda, which has become clear by the Vaikharydhvanis of 'ghaṭa', renders the meaning "ghaṭa' (pot), which is identified with it (the same Śabda) and does not express the meaning 'paṭa' (a cloth). The reason is that the Sphoṭaśabda does not have identity with the meaning 'paṭa'. On the other hand, since Sphoṭaśabda is only one, the meaning 'paṭa' should have been expressed by the Sphoṭaśabda exhibited by the Vaikharyśabda- 'ghaṭa'.

Therefore, the exhibited Sphoṭaśabda would be akin to the suggestive Vaikharydhvanis.

Intro : In case, the Sphoṭaśabda is exhibited through the suggestive speech-sounds, then such a Śabda would be of many types. Then the concept that – Śabda is eternal and single-would become untenable. Moreover, how can it be possible that the qualifies of sound, such as *sequence etc. are certainly exhibited in the Sphoṭaśabda* ? – the author clarifies the doubt –

नादस्य क्रमजन्मत्वात् न पूर्वो नापरश्च सः ।
अक्रमः क्रमरूपेण भेदवानिव जायते ।।

48. nādasya kramajanmatvāt na pūrvo nāparśca saḥ
akramaḥ kramarūpeṇa bhedavāniva jāyate

Sum : The Sphoṭaśabda is neither a 'previous' nor a 'subsequent'. It has got no sequence. But, since the Vaikhary (or speech-sound) has got some sequence, the Sphoṭa, which is revealed by Vaikhary, also seems as sequential and devided.

Com : In fact, the Sphoṭaśabda, which is there in the mind, is only one. It is neither previous nor subsequent. A thing, which has got previous and subsequent parts would have the said qualities.

The Sphoṭaśabda has got no parts. But the Vaikharyśabda, which illuminates the Sphoṭaśabda, has got its birth through the movement of lips etc. and it has got sequence. The same sequence can be attributed to a Sphoṭaśabda. Then such a Sphoṭaśabda may look like having sequence. So, the sequence experienced in the suggestive Vaikharydhvanis is attributed to the suggested Sphoṭaśabda and that'swhy the latter looks like having sequence.

Therefore, it is possible that the Sphoṭaśabda has originally got the qualities, singleness and eternity and through attribution of sequence, which is there in the suggestive sounds, got the quality of sequence too-it is possible.

Intro : The author *illustrates the concept of attribution of the quality of sequence*, which is there in speech sounds, to Sphoṭaśabda –

प्रतिबिम्बं यथान्यत्र स्थितं तोयक्रियावशात् ।
तत्प्रवृत्तिमिवान्वेति स धर्मः स्फोटनादयोः ।।

49. pratibimbam yathānyatra sthitam toyakriyāvaśāt
tatpravṛttimivānveti sa dharmaḥ sphoṭanādayoḥ

Sum : Just as a reflection formed elsewhere (water etc.) appears, due to the movement of water, to partake of the movement of the water, similar is the relationship between the Sphoṭa and Nāda.

Com : The speechsounds have got the qualities of short, long, previous and subsequent-the last being that of sequence. The Sphoṭaśabda is exhibited by such sounds. The said qualities of suggestive sounds are visible in the suggested Sphoṭaśabda. The quality of the image occurs in the reflection. The image of Moon reflects in water and that reflection naturally has got no quality such as movement. But the reflection gets such qualities from (the movement of) water. When water moves, the reflection of Moon also gets movement.

Intro : The author illustrates the *illumination of meaning by Śabda* –

आत्मरूपं यथा ज्ञाने ज्ञेयरूप च दृश्यते।
अर्थरूपं तथा शब्दे स्वरूपं च प्रकाशते।।

50. ātmarūpam yathā jñāne jneyarūpam ca dṛśyate
arth arūpam tathā śabde svarūpam ca prakāśate

Sum : Just as in the case of knowledge (both the knowledge and the object of knowledge or the thing), in Śabda too there appear both the meaning element and the formal element.

Com : When someone employs a sentence like 'ghaṭamānaya' (fetch the pot) then the listner gets the cognition 'fetch the pot'. Cognition (jñāna) means intelligence. (In summary the word 'knowledge' is used to denote jñāna). Such intelligence has got objects like 'ghaṭa' and 'paṭa (pot & cloth) as base. It cannot be independent of the objects. Interestignly, cognition/knowledge illuminates the objects and shines by itself too. A lamp is similar to cognition/knowledge – it illuminates the objects, so that they are visible to one's eyes and the lamp is visible too. In the same manner, a Śabda makes a subject-subject to knowledge and the knowledge by itself too would be the subject in the process. We comprehend the knowledge 'ghaṭa' by the Śabda 'ghaṭaḥ'. In such a knowledge, both, i.e. the object- 'pot' and the Śabda in the form of 'gh-a-ṭ-a-ḥ' are there unitedly. If the Śabda too does not appear, then only the image of knowledge such as 'ghaṭaḥ' (pot) is achieved. In case the Śabda too appears, the form of knowledge like 'the 'ghaṭa', meant by the Śabda 'ghaṭa' has to be exhibited.

Notes : The significatory power or 'Śakti' of Śabdas like 'ghaṭa' in expressing the form of the (same) Śabda, as in the case of meaning, has to be accepted. Generally, the Artha is the qualified and Śabda is the qualifier. The exception is in case of Śabdas such as 'kanyā' (virgin) and 'Agni' (fire) represented by Vyākaraṇasūtras. There it is the otherway round i.e., Śabda is qualified and Artha is qualifier.

Intro : It is claimed in verse 44, that Vaikharyvāk is the cause of Madhyamāvāk in the case of listner. For the speaker it is the otherway round, i.e. *Madhyam*āvāk is the cause of *Vaikharyvāk*. The author illustrates this concept –

आण्डभावमिवापन्नः यः क्रतुः शब्दसंज्ञकः।
वृत्तिस्तस्य क्रियारूपा भागशो भजते क्रमम्।।

51. āṇḍabhāvamivāpannaḥ yaḥ kratuḥ śabdasamjñakaḥ
vṛttistasya kriyārūpā bhāgaśo bhajate kramam

Sum : The sense (Buddhi) called Śabda exists like the essence in an egg. Its activity (āvirbhāva and tirobhāva) assumes sequence in every part (i.e. the Sphoṭa or Madhyamā is the cause of Vaikhary before one starts speaking, on the other hand the latter is the cause of the former when one listnes to a Śabda). After the union of birds of different sexes, the egg forms in the womb of the female bird and after some time the egg takes the shape of the bird.

Com : The Vaikharyvāk is the cause of Madhyamāvāk so far as the listner is concerned. But for a speaker the Madhyamāvāk is the cause of Vaikharyvāk. By the time the Vaikharyśabda with sequence, enters the mind of the listner, it would become single and without sequence. The same Śabda, while talking to others, appears to be sequential. Therefore, when we speak, the Vaikharyśabda is sequential but it looses its sequence and turns to a single form as soon as it enters the mind of the listner. The same Śabda, while talking to others, turn to be sequential. To sum up, while we are talking, the Vaikharyśabda is sequential. The same having entered the listner's mind, turns to be non-sequential. The same, while talking to others turns to be a sequential Vaikharyśabda-in this way the Śabda gets different forms. The process is illustrated through a Simili-birds like peahen are seen with good formation of different parts of the body.

This is the exploded view of a bird. When there is a sexual union between a peahen and peacock then the sperms of both the birds get mixed and get the shape of an egg in the womb of the peahen. There, in the egg is the fluid, which could in turn shape into a peahen/peacock. This is the amalgamated form of a bird. The same fluid, when hatched, would shape as a peacock/ peahen. This is the exploded view of the same bird. In the same manner a Śabda is also seen in three forms.

Notes : The word 'kratu' in Upaniṣads is seen in the sense of certainity. Following that, here in this verse it means 'Intelligence', (buddhi). Aṇḍaḥ means egg. The substance which is there in the egg is called 'Āṇḍaḥ' = the fluid., Bhāga means a part (of the body). It is followed by a 'śas', a Taddhita-suffix in Vīpsārtha. Vīpsā means pervasion.

Intro : We find sequence when a speaker utters a Śabda : But to the listner's mind it seems to be non-sequential and in a single form-this is the thesis proposed in earlier verses. The author *illustrates the same by offering another simili –*

यथैकबुद्धिविषया मूर्तिराक्रियते पटे।
मूर्त्यंतरस्य त्रितयमेवं शब्देऽपि दृश्यते।।

52. yathaikabuddhiviṣayā mūrtirākriyate paṭe
mūrtyantarasya tritayamevam śabdeépi dṛśyate

Sum : The painter first perceives the different parts of a shape and then gets a unified picture, then he paints the same on a cloth-likewise a Śabda has also got the three stages while comprehending.

Com : When a painter wants to do a man's picture, he firstly, identifies the man's limbs seperately. This is the exploded stage. Subsequently, without the difference of limbs, he forms general shape of the man in mind. This is the amalgamated second stage. Then the painter makes the man's picture, limb by limb, on a cloth or a paper, in the way he formerly identified. This is the exploded third stage. So much so that, the outer shape, the shape in the mind of the painter and the shape existing in the picture – three stages of the same form are seen. The Śabda would also have such three stages.
Notes : 'A single intellect is the subject to which' – thus when Bahuvrīhi is taken it is possible that the qualified, i.e. ekabuddhiviṣayā, can get the feminine gender in line with the qualifier, i.e. mūrtiḥ,.
Intro : The author again proves that *the Śabda exprsses its own form too –*

यथा प्रयोक्तुः प्राग् बुद्धिः शब्देष्वेव प्रवर्तते।
व्यवसायो ग्रहीतृणाम् एवं तेष्वेव जायते।।

53. yathā prayoktuḥ prāk buddhiḥ śabdeṣveva pravartate
vyavasāyo grahītṛāṇām evam teṣveva jāyate

Sum : Just as the mind of the speaker first considers the Śabdas only, the mind of the hearer first considers the Śabdas only.
Com : When a speaker wants to express his idea to others, then initially he tries to get the appropriate Śabdas (in the mind) and through them only conveys his thought.

The listner is he who understands through Śabdas. He initially applies his mind in Śabdas, and through them comprehends the meaning. It is a matter of common knowledge that without having known the form of Śabdas the listner cannot comprehend the meaning. Therefore, the Śabda would make the meaning as well as its form, subjct to intellect (jñāna). This verse elaborates the view already expressed in verse 51.
Notes : Initially, it is the meaning (Artha), which appears in the mind of the speaker. In accordance with the meaning only, he discerns Śabdas. Following this, first it is the Artha and next Śabda, which appear in the mind of the speaker. But this verse is not written following this sequence. Rather, it is written taking, the process while a speaker expresses his ideas, into account. According to this process, it is the Śabdas and not the meanings which appear initially in the mind of the speaker.
Intro : Śabda is a particular instrument in the expression of meaning. It means that the Śabda 'ghaṭaḥ' (pot) creates the cognition related to the meaning. Moreover, it is claimed that it makes its form of 'GH-A-Ṭ-A-Ḥ', subject to the

cognition. There is the doubt : in day to day life when somebody says 'ghaṭamānaya' (fetch the pot) the listner brings the pot, when it is said 'eat the rice', the listner eats the rice. Here, in the above sentences, the meanings of 'ghaṭa' and 'rice' have got connection (syntactic and semantic) with the verbs. In the same manner, Why is it that the Śabdas are also expressed, i.e. when the meaning as well as the form of the Śabda are expressed by the Śabda, then on a par with the meaning, the Śabda too must have connection with the verb – *the author clarifies the doubt* –

अर्थोपसर्जनीभूतानभिधेयेषु केषुचित् ।
चरितार्थान् परार्थत्वान्न लोकः प्रतिपद्यते ।।

54. arthopasarjanībhūtānabhidheyeṣu keṣucit
caritārthān parārthatvānna lokaḥ pratipadyate

Sum : Speakers – when certain meanings are conveyed, (the forms) or Śabdas – having become accessories to the meaning and having their purpose served, they are not perceived as accessories to action, as they are meant for the sake of another thing (i.e. meaning).

Cam : People, when think of conveying the ideas in their minds, employ Śabdas as the instruments. In doing so, the conveying of meaning is important. Since it is useful as an instrument in the process, the Śabda is unimportant. One, who wants to have a meal would use plate etc. as instruments. Śabdas are similar to these instruments. Therefore, since they are unimportant people do not connect the Śabdas (fetching etc.) with the verbs.

Notes : Sometimes it is found that some Śabdas, which are not unimportant are connected with the verbs. In Vyākaraṇa certain applications are imposed upon pronounced Śabdas, such as Kanyā and Agni. Such Śabdas have got connection with the applicatons.

Intro : Śabda illuminates the meaning as well as its own form – it is stated in verse 50. It means that Śabda would be both causing perception as well as being perceived. There is a doubt – *it is not possible to have both the qualities of illuminator and illuminated,* which are incompatible ? – the author clarifies –

ग्राह्यत्वं ग्राहकत्वं च द्वे शक्ती तेजसो यथा ।
तथैव सर्वशब्दानामेते पृथगवस्थिते ।।

55. grāhyatvam grāhakatvam ca dve śaktī tejaso yathā
tathaiva sarvaśabdānāmete pṛthagavasthite

Sum : just as the light has two capacities, viz. that of being perceived and of causing perception of objects, all Śabdas have got these two distinct capacities.

Com : A pronounced Śabda would convey the meaning and hence it is called 'grāhaka' (one which causes grasping). So it is clear that the Śabda has got the capacity to cause perception. While grasping the meaning, the Śabda along with Artha would also become subject in knowledge. Therefore, it can be said that the Śabda has got the capacity of being grasped (grāhyatva).

Light can be the best example to explain the above said process, which is explained in verse 50. Knowledge is taken as an example there. In other words—knowledge, light and Śabda belong to the same category. They are illuminators of other objects as well as themselves. Therefore, the qualities of being perceived and causing perception of objects as well as being illuminated and causing illumination are there in all these three things.

Notes : Objects like pot etc. are perceived, they cannot cause perception. Sence-organs, like eye and ear, cause grasping, but cannot be perceived. Even when analysed in such a way it is clear that both the said qualities are incompatible. On the other hand, since both the qualities are noticed in light and knowledge, the compatibility is not unnatural.

Both the capacities are there in a Śabda in an indivisible form. But the difference is felt due to the functions. This view is suggested by the word 'iva' (like).

Intro : The author explains the benefit of the above proposition accepting that *there are two capacities in a Śabda*—

विषयत्वमनापन्नैः शब्दैर्नार्थः प्रकाश्यते ।
न सत्तयैव तेऽर्थानामगृहीताः प्रकाशकाः ।।

56. viṣayatvamanāpannaiḥ śabdairnārthaḥ prakāśyate
na sattayaiva teérthānāmagṛhītāḥ prakāśakāḥ

Sum : Some things are capable of creating activity although they are not known-by taste or touch, for example-sugar and fire. On the otherhand, meaning is not understood from Śabdas, which have not become objects. They do not, without being received, express meaning by their mere existence.

Com : Some things in the world fulfill their action even without the knowledge as to what that particular thing is. Sugar can be tasted even without prior knowledge that the thing being tasted is sugar. One would get his hand burnt if he touches fire, with or without the knowledge that the thing being touched is fire. Likewise, the sense-organs, like eye and ear, generate knowledge. All the said things fulfill their functions by their mere existance.

Śabda is not like that—unless and until one has got the specific form—that this is the word 'pot'—and unless the same becomes subject to knowledge—he cannot grasp the meaning (of the word). In short, a Śabda does not convey the meaning by its mere existence. The sense-organ —ear, catches the Varṇas (phonemes). The phonemes cannot convey the meaning. The Śabda exhibited by the phonemes can convey the meaning. Since Śabda is also the subject of knowledge it has become possible as the existence of two types of capacities in Śabda is accepted.

Intro : The meaning is understood only when the specific form of Śabda that -this is the word pot-is known : the *author substantiates this concept* by giving another reason –

अतोऽनिर्ज्ञातरूपत्वात् किमाहेत्यभिधीयते ।
नेन्द्रियाणां प्रकाश्येऽर्थे स्वरूपं गृह्यते तथा ।।

57. ato 'nirjñātarūpatvāt kimāhetyabhidhīyate
nendriyāṇām prakāśye 'rthe svarūpam gṛhyate tathā

Sum : Therefore, when the form of the pronounced Śabda is not known the question –'what did you say ?' is being asked. But the nature of the sense-organs is not similarly (like Śabda in denoting the meaning) grasped, when an object has to be revealed by them.

Com : The meaning is understood after the Śabda is uttered. In truth, a careful thinking concludes that a meaning cannot be understood by the mere utterance of Śabda. The Śabda has to be grasped. To prove this fact the non-existence of Śabda is much helpful when uttered, since the Śabda is grasped, the meaning is understood. But when a speaker utters a sentence like-fetch the pot-and the listner could not hear the same, the latter would/could not fetch the pot. Consequently, the listner would ask-what did you say ? On the other hand, in case the Śabda is not grasped, still it has expressed the meaning, then the above question would have not arisen. Moreover, when the speaker utteres the same Śabda loudly and clearly, then, since the Śabda is grasped, the listner gets the knowledge.

Notes : The sense-organs (eye, ear etc.) are not like the Śabda. The idea is elaborated under verse 56.

Intro : In verse 55 it is proposed that the Śabda has got two types of capacities. In this verse, *the author discusses the role of the capacities* in regard with Vyākaraṇaśāstra –

भेदेनावगृहीतौ द्वौ शब्दधर्मावपोद्धृतौ ।
भेदकार्येषु हेतुत्वमविच्छेदेन गच्छतः ।।

58. bhedenavagṛhitau dvau śabdadharmāvapoddhṛtau
bhedakāryeṣu hetutvamavicchedena gacchataḥ

Sum : The said two aspects of Śabda (grāhyatva and grāhakatva), which are analysed and seperated by mind, act without mutual opposition as causes of different effects (like the relation of saṃjñā and saṃjñī).

Com : Bheda means difference. The relation between meanings (of Śabdas) is based on difference. At some places in Vyākaraṇa, a single Śabda is considered as having the relation of Saṃjñā and Saṃjñī (or name and the named). In order to adjust such consideration a single capacity is shown (described) in two different types. A Śabda is considered to be different due to the difference in capacity. Such Śabdas are considered to be both a Samjñā and Samjñī. In case, the difference in capacity is not established the same Śabda cannot have the said relation of Samjñā and Samjñī. Samjñā is an instrument in identifying a thing or person. The person or thing being identified is Samjñī. For example – Rāma, Bhīma, Nala etc. are Samjñīs. They are in the form of human beings. Here the relation of Samjñā and Samjñī is felt since the difference between the forms of Samjñā and Samjñī is clearly visible.

In Vyākaraṇaūtras a Śabda (single) is considered to have got the relation of Samjñā and Samjñī. There, a single Śabda has become devided for being the common base of two capacities. Both such Śabdas have got the said relation. The Śabda with the quality of 'grāhakatva' is considered as Samjñā and the other Śabda with the quality of 'grāhyatva' as Samjñī. When the said procedure is followed then there won't be different qualties at a single point. Consequently, the paradox has gone and the Samjñā-Samjñī relation is retained.

Notes : Verse 60 would illustrate the concept in this verse.

Intro : The author wants to *illustrate the proposition made in verse 58, and in that connection quotes Vṛ*ddhi etc. as examples –

वृद्ध्यादयो यथा शब्दाः स्वरूपोपनिबन्धनाः ।
आदैच्प्रत्यायितैश्शब्दैः सम्बन्धं यान्ति संज्ञिभिः ।।

59. vṛddhyādayo yathā śabdāḥ svarūpopanibandhanāḥ
ādaicpratyāyitaiśśabdaiḥ sambandham yānti samjñibhiḥ

Sum : Just as the word Vṛddhi and the like, besides expressing their own form are also related to the sounds named by them (i.e. ā, ai and au).

Com : Pāṇini's first Sūtra, viz. 'Vṛddhirādaic', enjoins that the phonemes, ā-ai-au, are called Vṛddhi. The Śabda 'Vṛddhi' is a Samjñā. The phonemes denoted by the word 'ādaic' are Samjñīs. Here both Samjñā and Samjñī are naturally different. Therefore, the relation between both the factors is effected with ease.

On the other hand, the relation of Samjñā and Samjñī has to be applied in a single Śabda. In fact, there are no two different Śabdas. So difference in Śabdas has to be created through difference in quality. So much so that, in both the instances having natural or created difference, the relation of Samjñā and Samjñī can be applied. The same idea is explained in this verse. There are several instances where different Śabdas have got the relation of Samjñā and samjñī. The point to note is that the Samjñāśabda denotes the Śabda only. Ādaic are called Vṛddhi – is the general meaning. Ādaic' are not different from Vṛddhi (ādaicaḥ Vṛddhipadābhinnaḥ is the primary meaning Vācyārtha). This fact is explained in verse 66.

Notes : In this verse the word Śabdaḥ denotes the Samjñā and the other one, Śabdaiḥ denotes the Samjñiśabda.

Intro : The author applies the *simili in an example* –

अग्निशब्दस्तथैवायमग्निशब्दनिबन्धनः ।
अग्निश्रुत्यैति संबन्धमग्निशब्दाभिधेयया ।।

60. agniśabdastathaivāyamagniśabdanibandhanaḥ
agniśṛtyaiti sambandhamagniśabdābhidheyayā

Sum : Similarly, (in line with Śabdas like Vṛddhi etc.) the Śabda 'agni' in the maxim 'Agnerḍhak' (4-2-33), which has got the Śabda 'agni' as pravṛttinimitta (cause in activity), would get the relation of Samjñā and Samjñī, with the Śabda-agni in the example denoted by the Śabda-agni in the same Sūtra.

Com : In the sense, 'agni is the God of this' (oblation), 'ḍhak', a 'taddhita-pratyaya' is applied to agniśabda (agnerḍhak -Pāṇini-4-2-33). After completion of the entire application the Śabda 'āgneyam' is formed. Here the Śabda 'agni' in the example, is indicated by the Śabda 'agni' in the Sūtra and the suffix is effected to the former. So much so that, the agni - Śabda in the Sūtra is Samjñā and the one in the example is Samjñī, the relation being that between a Samjñā and a Samjñī. It's conspicuous that in the above context the same Śabda has got the relation. Such a relation was possible due to the creation of difference in the same Śabda in the form of grāhyatva and grāhakatva.

Notes : Pāṇini has indicated the relation of Samjñā and Samjñī in such Sūtras through the Sūtra-svam rūpam śabdasyāśabdasamjñā (1-1-68). The Sūtra says that the very form of the Śabda would be the Samjñī. Consequently, since there is grāhyatva in it, the Śabda would be Samjñī and due to grāhakatva it would be Samjñā too. In Vyākaraṇa, whereever some application is enjoined by pronouncing certain Śabda the same regulation is effected. Another example is -kanyāyāḥ kanīna ca (4-1-116- Pāṇini)-kanyāyāḥ apatyam pumān kānīnaḥ (the son of a virgin is called kānīnaḥ), Vyāsa and Karṇa are kānīnas. In Astādhyāyī, there are many Sūtras of this type.

In this verse there are four Agniśabdas – 1. the one is the Sūtra, 2. the one which says the first one in Śabdapravṛttinimittaka (that was the cause in employing the Śabda), 3. the one which indicates the Agniśabda in the example, 4. the one which says that the Agniśabda in the example is denoted by the one in the Sūtra. This verse illustrates the concepts of both the verses 58 and 59.

Intro : Let the applications enjoined by the Sūtras may not be effected to the meaning, but why is it that *they are not effected even to the Śabdas pronounced in the Sūtras ?* the author answers the question—

योयं उच्चार्यते शब्दः नित्यं न स कार्यभाक्।
अन्यप्रत्यायने शक्तिः अन्यस्य प्रतिबध्यते।।

61. yo ya uccāryate śabdo nityam na sa kāryabhāk
anyapratyāyane śaktiranyasya pratibadhyate

Sum : Whichever Śabda is uttered in the Sūtra does not necessarily get the grammatical operation. Nor the capacity of the Śabda in conveying other form is obstructed.

Com : The agniśabda in the Sūtra 'agnerḍhak' is useful in generating the congnition of agniśabda in the example and thus in effecting the application of the suffix to the same. This is the purpose meant by the pronouncement of agni śabda in the above Sūtra. Therefore, since it is pronounced for other purpose (than getting the application of the suffix to it), and hence it became unimportant, the application enjoined by the Sūtra is not effected to the same Śabda. The application is effected to the one which is there in the example. The Śabda pronounced in the Sūtra may not get the suffix enjoined by the same Sūtra. But since there won't be any objection, it denotes the Śabda in the example.

Notes : This is the sole purpose of all the Samjñāsūtras. Having denoted the Samjñī, they remain neutral. Since Samjñī is important, the applications are effected to that and since the Samjñā is unimportant, no application is effected to that.

Intro : The author explains as to *why the applications are not effected to* the Śabdas pronounced in the Sūtras—

उच्चरन् परतन्त्रत्वात् गुणः कार्यैर्न युज्यते।
तस्मात्तदर्थैः कार्याणाम् सम्बन्धः परिकल्प्यते।।

62. uccaran paratantratvād guṇaḥ karyairna yujyate
tasmāttadarthaiḥ kāryāṇām sambandhaḥ parikalpyate

Sum : The Śabda pronounced in Sūtra is for the sake of the thing meant, hence secondary. Therefore, it is not concerned with grammatical operations. So the same operations are attached to the Śabdas denoted by those in the Sūtra.

Com : The Śabda pronounced in the Sūtra is meant for somethingelse, (to denote the Śabda in the example), and hence it is secondary. Therefore it does not get any application. On the other hand, since the Śabda, which is there in the example, is primary the applications are effected to it.

Notes : In this verse, the word 'uccaran' means 'uccāryamāṇa'. The latter indicates the sense of urge and thus the above meaning is attained. The word 'guṇa' means secondary.

Intro : The Śabda in the Sūtra is secondary as it is for the sake of denoting the Śabda in the example. Therefore, the application is not effected to that Śabda – it is explained in verse 62. Then, since the Śabda in the example is pronounced for the sake of understanding by human beings, the same is also secondary, and therefore the application cannot be effected to such a Śabda too – the author before going to answer this question, in verse 65 *gives an illustration* –

सामान्यमाश्रितं यद्यदुपमानोपमेययोः ।
तस्य तस्योपमानेषु धर्मोऽन्यो व्यतिरिच्यते ।।

63. sāmānyamāśritam yadyadupamānopameyayoḥ
tasyatasyopamāneṣu dharmo'nyo vyatiricyate

Sum : Whichever common attributes there exist in the object with which anything is compared and the thing which is compared to it, some attributes other than these also exist in the object to which comparison is made.

Com : It is commonly said that the face (of the heroin) is as beautiful as the Moon. So the relation of upamāna (the thing brought for comparison) and upameya (the thing being compared) is felt. The reason for this is the difference between two things. The beauty is the common feature. It is there in both in the same form. Since the face and Moon are naturally different, the beauty which is there in both of them is also different. Therefore, as it is in the case of face and Moon, the relation of Upamāna and Upameya has to be effected, between both the beauties. Then some common feature like glittering has to be applied. In case one wishes to say (vivakṣā) that the said common feature is different due to the difference in resort (āśraya) another common feature has to be created. So much so that, the creation of common feature is an endless process. It depends on the wish to say or Vivakṣā

Notes : In the same manner the sentence-Kṣatriya is reciting like a Brāhmaṇa- has to be analysed. In this sentence Brāhmaṇa is Upamāna and Kṣatriya is Upameya. Recitation (regular) is the common feature. The feature is one but Brāhmaṇa and Kṣatriya are different. Therefore, their recitation is different too. Then in case one draws analogy between the two recitations, the common feature would be perfection. If the same perfection is treated as different there would be another common feature and thus it is an endless process.

The purpose of such creation of common features would be clear in verse 65.

Intro : The author offers *another example* –

गुणः प्रकर्षहेतुर्यः स्वातन्त्र्येणोपदिश्यते।
तस्याश्रितादगुणादेव प्रकृष्टत्वं प्रतीयते।।

64. guṇaḥ prakarṣaheturyaḥ svatantryeṇopadiśyate
tasyāśritādguṇādeva prakṛṣṭatvam pratīyate

Sum : Whatever quality, which is the cause of excellence (of an object) is (itself) mentioned in the form of an object, its (own) excellence is caused by the qualities residing in it.

Com : In order to express the degrees of comparison both the suffixes 'tara' and 'tama'-are employed. Example – śuklataraḥ paṭaḥ, śuklatamaḥ paṭaḥ. The speaker means this cloth is whiter/whitest. Naturally the cloth does not have any degrees of utkarṣa or apakarṣa. Rather depending on the degree of whiteness, which is there in the thing/object (cloth), it became possible to call the cloth whiter/whitest. Moreover, the suffix 'tarap' applies depending on the degree of 'śuklarūpa' in the sentence, 'śuklataraḥ paṭah', whereas the same suffix indicates the degree of Śuklatva in the sentence ['paśya] rūpam śuklataram' (see, the form of the cloth is whiter). In the said process the creation of common features can be effected like a chain. It all depends on the wish of the speaker (vivakṣā).

Verse 65 speaks of the purpose of such a creation.

Intro : Two concepts were proposed in the earlier two verses. Now the author goes on to describe *their purpose in the present context* –

तस्याभिधेयभावेन यः शब्दः समवस्थितः।
तस्याप्युच्चारणे रूपमन्यत्तस्माद्विविच्यते।।

65. tasyābhidheyabhāvena yaḥ śabdaḥ samavasthitaḥ
tasyāpyuccāraṇe rūpamanyattasmādvivicyate

Sum : When a word, which has its own form as its meaning, is pronounced then the Śabda in the example is discriminated from the same. (in the Sūtra 'agnerḍhak' – the meaning of the word 'agni', i.e. agni, is taken distinctly).

Com : In order to denote the Śabda in the example, the Śabda in the Sūtra is pronounced. Therefore, the latter is unimportant. The suffix imposed by the Sūtra appliees to the Śabda in the example. Since the Śabda in the Sūtra is unimportant, the suffix does not apply to the same. The reason here is pronouncement. This concept was discussed in verse 62.

Here is a clarification to the doubt raised in the introduction to verse 63 – Both the Śabdas are absolutely different. Therefore, it is possible that the imposed application is effected to either Śabda. When the merit of pronouncement is common to both the Śabdas how is it that the application is effected to only one and not the other ? The answer to this question is – yes, but they differ from each other due to the difference in the act of pronouncement. The pronouncement of Agniśabda in the example is different from that of the same in the Sūtra. The difference in the effect is caused by the difference in action. So much so that, the Śabda, that is uttered for effecting an application won't receive the same. A different application may be effected. The Agniśabda in the Sūtra is uttered for effecting the suffix 'ḍhak'. Therefore, the same suffix is not effected to the same Śabda (i.e. the one in the Sūtra). But such a Śabda can denote the Śabda with the same form in the example. The 'Agniśabda' in the example is pronounced in order to denote the relation with oblation. The same Śabda would get the suffix 'ḍhak'.

Notes : Two examples are given in versees 62 & 64 to clarify the doubt as to whether the difference created in the above manner is justified. The justification is as in the case of 'face is beautiful like Moon' and 'śuklataraḥ paṭaḥ', which are examples for simili and the suffix 'tarap'. All this is possible depending on the speaker's desire to express (vivakṣā).

Intro : Here is an *explanation* of the term 'bhedakāryeṣu' (verse 58) –

प्राक्संज्ञिनाभिसंबन्धात् संज्ञा रूपपदार्थिका ।
षष्ठयाश्च प्रथमायाश्च निमित्तत्वाय कल्पते ।।

66. prāksamjñinābhisambandhāt samjñā rūpapadārthikā
ṣaṣṭhyāśca prathamāyāśca nimittatvāya kalpate

Sum : Before being connected to the thing it means, a name is capable of possessive and nominative cases, because it has its own form as its meaning.

Com : In Vyākaraṇaśāstra, the Śabda 'Vṛddhi' denotes ā, ai, and au as Pāṇini says 'Vṛddhirādaic' (1-1-1). But this is possible only after the meaning of the above Sūtra is conceived. So much so that at the time of the conception of the Samjñāsūtra (Vṛddhirādaic), the Śabda – 'Vṛddhi' cannot denote the vowels – ā, ai, and au. During that time 'Vṛddhi' means the form of the word 'Vṛddhi' and not 'development' as it generally means. The latter meaning is not applicable in the present context. Therefore, like 'ghaṭa' means a pot, 'Vṛddhi' means the form of the same word, consisting the phonemes – V-Ṛ-D-DH-I.

Notes : In Vyākaraṇa, there are two types of Samjñāsūtras-1. Both the terms denoting Samjñā and Samjñī are in nominative case ; example : Vṛddhirādaic (Pāṇini 1-1-1). Here the Vṛddhiśabda is Samjñā and ādaic are Samjñīs. Both are in nominative case. 2. The term indicating Samjñā is in nominative case whereas the Samjñī is in possessive case; example : Uñaḥ (Pāṇini 1-1-17). This Sūtra says that the Nipāta – 'uñ', when followed by the word 'iti' would get the Pragṛhyasamjñā. Here the Samjñī – 'uñ' is in possessive case. Samjñā is in

(...pragṛhyam, 1-1-11) nominative case. Therefore, the Samjñī would be in both nominative and possessive cases.

In this verse the word 'Padārtha' is synonymous to 'vācyārtha'. Rūpa means 'svarūpa' (the form). That is a Bahuvrīhi compound – rūpam padārthaḥ yasyāḥ sā (which word has got its form as the meaning).

Intro : The author explains as to *how the nominative* and objective cases are *applicable* –

तत्रार्थवत्वात् प्रथमा संज्ञाशब्दाद्विधीयते।
अस्येति व्यतिरेकश्च तदर्थादेव जायते।।

67. tatrārthavatvātprathamā samjñāśabdādvidhīyate
asyeti vyatirekaśca tadarthādeva jāyate

Sum : The nominative is prescribed to a name because it is meaningful with its form and it is from the same meaning that the possessive construction in the form 'to this' arises.

Com : The Samjñāśabda denotes its form, when it is not mixed with the Samjñī. Therefore, such a Śabda would be meaningful and gets the Prātipadikasamjñā and consequently the nominative case.

Notes : In case the difference between the Samjñā and Samjñī is not intended then both would be in nominative case. Examples : Vṛddhirādaic (1-1-1) and Bhūvādayo Dhātavaḥ (1-3-11). When, on the other hand the difference is intended then the possessive case to Samjñī would be correct. It results in a form like 'ādaicām Vṛddhiḥ' (Vṛddhisamjñā will be there for ā, ai and au).

Uñaḥ – can be offered as an example for possessive case.

Intro : Until now the author discussed the Sūtra-svam rūpam śabdasyāśabdasamjñā, in light of the two factors i.e. grāhyatva and grāhakatva. Now *he applies the relation of Samjñā and Samjñī*, depending on the difference of Jāti (class) and Vyakti (individual) aspects, to the same Sūtra.

स्वं रूपमिति कैश्चित्तु व्यक्तिस्संज्ञोपदिश्यते।
व्यक्तेः कार्याणि संसृष्टा जातिस्तु प्रतिपद्यते।।

68. svam rūpamiti kaiścittu vyaktissamjñopadiśyate
vyakteḥ kāryāṇi samsṛṣṭā jātistu pratipadyate

Sum : Some are of the view that name as a particular/ individual (Vyakti) is meant in the Sūtra – svam rūpam śabdasyāśabdasamjñā, but that is the Universal/Class (Jāti), having permanent relation with individual, which undergoes grammatical operations.

Com : Right from verse 58 till now the author discussed the Sūtra-svam rūpam śabdasyāśabdasamjñā, in light of both the capacities, i.e. grāhyatva and grāhakatva, that a Śabda possesses. The purport of the discussion was that one has to accept the difference in the Śabda and through that the relation of Samjñā and Samjñī is to be evolved. On the otherhand, in order to show the relation of Samjñā and Samjñī in accordance with Jāti and Vyakti theories, the author has written three verses – 68, 69 & 70.

Śabdas like Agni and Kanyā are there in both Sūtras as well as examples. As there is ghaṭatvajāti in a ghaṭa, there is Agnitvajāti and kanyātvajāti in the above Śabdas. So much so that the Śabda consisting of the phonemes – a-g-n-i-is called Vyakti where as the Agniśabdatva, which is there in the same Śabda is taken as Jāti.

In this verse the author exhibits the thesis of certain people that the Śabdavyakti in the Śabdas in Vyākaraṇasūtras is Samjñā and the Śabdatvajāti in the Śabdas in the example is Samjñī.

In case the Agniśabdatvajāti is Samjñī, the suffixes etc. cannot be applied to it. Rather the Vyakti has got a permanently fixed relation with Jāti. Vyakti gets the application and through that the Jāti.

Intro : In the earlier verse the author has given the opinion of some philosophers that the Vyakti is Samjñā and the Jāti is the Samjñī. Here he shows that *the Vyakti is Samjñī and Jā*ti is Samjñ*ā* –

संज्ञिनीं व्यक्तिमिच्छन्ति सूत्रग्राह्यामथापरे ।
जातिप्रत्यायिता शक्तिः प्रदेशेषूपजायते ।।

69. saṃjñinim vyaktimicchanti sūtragrāhyāmathāpare
jātipratyāyitā śaktiḥ pradeśeṣūpajāyate

Sum : Others take a position that which is meant by the Sūtra, viz. svam rūpam śabdasyaśabdasamjñā, is a particular instance of the named (and that it is the Class which is named) and that in any given instance one finds only a particular/individual, the understanding of which is brought about by the Universal/Class.

Com : Two theses were given in verse 68 & 69, since there is no any regulation which stipulates that either must be the Samjñī and not the other. Neither affects the grammatical function. Nevertheless, in order to sharpen the brains through attributing importance and non-importance to Jāti and Vyakti, Bhartrhari has related the arguments.

Intro : The author *substantiates the relation of Samjñā and samjñī* depending on Jāti and Vyakti, proposed in verses 68 & 69 –

कार्यत्वे नित्यताया वा केचिदेकत्ववादिनः ।
कार्यत्वे नित्यतायां वा केचिन्नानात्ववादिनः ।।

70. kāryatve nityatāyām vā kecidekatvavādinaḥ
kāryatve nityatāyām vā kecinnānātvavādinaḥ

Sum : Both among those who uphold the eternity theory of Śabdas and those who hold that Śabdas are created – there are some who uphold its sameness (only one Śabda not many). On the otherhand among the upholders of the doctrine of eternity and of the doctrine that Śabdas are created there are those who uphold the plurality of Śabdas (i.e. that every occurence of the same Śabda is the occurence of diferent Śabda).

Com : Even if a Śabda has got so many meanings, there will be only a single Śabda (not many). We are not concerned with the argument as to whether a Śabda is eternal or non-eternal. In both the cases the Śabda will be only one – this is the opinion of a group of philosophers. So much so that there won't be Jāti according to these people. Jāti is applicable when there are many individuals (vyaktis). Therefore, in accordance with the above concept, one should not interpret the Sūtra 'svam rūpam śabdasyāśabdasamjñā by applying the Jāti and Vyakti. Sūtra, 'Svam rūpam' can be interpreted in accordance with the Jati and Vyakti.

Intro : In continuation of the discussion about the eternity of Śabda, the author *explains the view of Mīmāmsakas* (who accept the eternity of Śabda) in regard to a phoneme, word and sentence –

पदभेदेऽपि वर्णानामेकत्वं न निवर्तते ।
वाक्येषु पदमेकं च भिन्नेष्वप्युपलभ्यते ।।

71. padabhede' pi varṇānāmekatvam na nivartate
vākyeṣu padamekam ca bhinneṣvapyupalabhyate

Sum : Even when the word is a different one, the identity of the letters is not impaired, and (in the same way) in different sentences the same word is observed (this is the doctrine of Mīmāmsakas, who argue that letters are eternal and both the word and the sentence are a myth)

Com : There are different words like 'arkaḥ' (sun) and 'aśvaḥḥ' (horse). There are four phonemes in these words collectively. They are not different from each other. Place does not cause the difference between two (or more) phonemes. Their form is identified as one and the same. The 'r' and 'ṭ' in the words 'arka'. 'markaṭa' and 'karkaṭa' are one and the same. The 'a', 'i', 'r', etc. across the speech are one and the same. Of course, 'a' is different from 'i'. The phonemes are not created. They are eternal.

Moreover, although, the sentences look to be different, the words there, with the same form, won't loose their oneness. They all are the same. 'Fetch the pot'. 'look at the photo', 'fetch the horse', 'look at the cow' – such sentences are different. But, the words there, in the same form, i.e. 'fetch', 'lookat', are non-different.

Notes : Therefore, there is not a sentence different from words nor a word differennt from phonemes. Phonemes themselves are words and the latter themselves are sentences. 'Gauḥ' – what is the Śabda here ? The answer for this question will be – 'G + AU + :'. So much so that phonemes are the very candidates. Words and sentences are created, and therefore illusory.

Intro : The author *elaborates* the same concept –

न वर्णव्यतिरेकेण पदमन्यच्च विद्यते ।
वाक्यं वर्णपदाभ्यां च व्यतिरिक्तं न किंचन

72. na varṇavyatirekeṇa padamanyacca vidyate
vākyam varṇapadābhyām ca vyatiriktam na kiñcana

Sum : Therefore, the word does not exist as more than its phonemes, nor is there a sentence existing as more than the phonemes and the words.

Com : The theory of Naiyāyikas that a group of phonemes is a word and that of words is a sentence, cannot be substantiated. Therefore, phonemes are genuine and words and sentences are nothing but illusion.

Intro : Continuing his discussion about the eternity of Śabdas, Bhartṛhari puts forth *his* (*Grammarians*') theory, simultaneously *refuting the Mīmāmsakas*' view –

पदे न वर्णा विद्यन्ते वर्णेष्ववयवा न च ।
वाक्यात्पदानामत्यन्तं प्रविवेको न कश्चन ।।

73. pade na varṇā vidyante varṇeṣvavayavā na ca
vākyātpadānāmatyantam praviveko na kaścana

Sum : Just as there are no parts in phonemes, there are no phonemes in a word. Nor is there any reality in abstracting the words from a sentence.

Com : Meaning can be expressed only through a sentence. That is the only genuine candidate. Words and phonemes are extracted from that. Therefore, they are illusory. This concept was related in verse 24.

The phoneme 'ṛ' appears to have consisted of two 'r' s. In truth, they are not there. Similarly in a word like 'ghaṭa', phonemes like 'gh' etc. seem to be existing. They are not there. They were created and hence the appearence. Word is indivisible.

After careful consideration it seems that the sentence is the real unit. Words look like parts of sentence. It was due to creation. Words do not exist in the least. Sentence is indivisible. The same only renders an indivisible meaning.

Notes : Therefore, neither the theory of Mīmāmsakas that only phonemes are real, nor that of Naiyāyikas that words only are real-can be taken for granted. Rather, both the above theories are replica of the artificial arrangements made by the Vaiyākaraṇas for the purpose of grammatical applications (attributing meaning to suffixes, words etc.)

Here in this verse the word 'na' denotes similarity and not negation as is the case generally. In some texts 'iva' is seen in place of 'naca'.

Intro : 'Both the above concepts are there in currency' – asserts the author –

भिन्नं दर्शनमाश्रित्य व्यवहारोऽनुगम्यते ।
तत्र यन्मुख्यमेकेषां तत्रान्येषां विपर्ययः ।।

74. bhinnam dars'anamās'ritya vyavaāro'nugamyate
tat'ra yanmukhyamekeṣām tatrānyeṣām viparyayaḥ

Sum : In practice the followers of every system follow a different theory. The doctrine which is important to one side is totally unacceptable to others. (Vaiyākaraṇas believe in a sentence but for grammatical operations they take up a word. Similarly, the Mīmāmsakas hold that only letters are true but take up a sentence and try to interpret the same).

Com : The Vaiyākaraṇas who contend that only sentence is the real unit (others are artificial), carry on their grammatical applications taking phonemes, morphemes and words (and attributing meaning to them). Without phonemes morphemes and words such applications are simply impossible. On the other hand, the Mīmāmsakas whose contention is that only phonemes are real (others, i.e. words and sentences are artificial) take up words and sentences in Vedic exegeses.

Then how to resolve this problem ? – the latter part of the verse is said in answer to this question-interestingly, all the philosophers apply all the theories. Otherwise the S'āstras would become null and void. Rather, each side considers either theory to be important and the rest as secondary. Mīmāmsakas hold that phoneme is real and the rest are secondary, whereas Vaiyākaraṇas maintain that sentence is real and phonemes and words are secondary.

Intro : In verse 23 it was pronounced, that the relation between Śabda and Artha is eternal. What is a Śabda ? How is it that it is eternal ? – both these questions are answered in verse 44 by describing the Sphoṭas'abda and Vaikharys'abda. The result of the discussion was that the Sphoṭs'abda is eternal. In the same context, while answering the question as to how the Sphoṭas'abda renders the meaning, (incidentally) the relation of Samjñā and Samjñī, the singularity and plurality of Śabda etc. are discussed.

Presently, the author answers the question as to – when due to the difference in time the Śabda becomes non-eternal, *how can the eternity of Śabda be substantiated ?* –

स्फोटस्याभिन्नकालस्य ध्वनिकालानुपातिनः ।
ग्रहणोपाधिभेदेन वृत्तिभेदं प्रचक्षते ।।

75. sphoṭasyābhinnakālasya dhvanikālānupātinaḥ
grahaṇopādhibhedena vṛttibhedam pracakṣāte

Sum : Patañjali says that the Sphoṭa, which is not divided by time, but adopts the time of Vaikharydhvāni, gets the difference of Vṛttis (i.e. hrasvadīrghaplutas or drutamadhyavilambitas) due to the adoptation of the properties of mind or Vaikharydhvani.

Com : Since Sphoṭaśabda is eternal, it does not receive the qualities of time, like plurality and non-eternity. Only non-eternal things are time-bound. The Vaikhary-sounds suggest the Sphoṭaśabda. The latter follows the time of the former. It is not possible to find Sphoṭaśabda apart from the Vaikhary-sounds.

Through mind or (Vaikhary) sounds the difference of hrasva, dīrgha and pluta in the Sphoṭaśabda is felt. The phonemes with one, two and three seconds duration are called hrasva, dīrgha and pluta (short, long and prolated vowels) respectively. Similarly, while speaking or reading – if nine drops flow out of Suṣumnānāḍi it is called drutavṛtti, and if the flow is twelve and sixteen drops it is called Madhyavṛtti and Vilambitavṛṭti, respectively. A poem can be read slowly, fast and faster. These three situations are identified with three Vṛttis. These three Vṛittis are not there in the Sphoṭaśabda. They are the qualities of Upādhi. Mind or Vaikharydhvani can be the Upādhi here. One which adopts its qualities to another is called Upādhi.

So much so that naturally the Sphoṭaśabda, which is suggested is one and eternal and the differences of hrasva etc. are due to the difference in the suggestive sound – this is the purport of the verse.

Intro : The author *substantiates* the idea expressed in verse 75 –

स्वभावभेदान्नित्यत्वे ह्रस्वदीर्घप्लुतादिषु ।
पाकृतस्य ध्वनेः कालः शब्दस्येत्युपचर्यते ।।

76. svabhāvabhedānnityatve hrasvadīrghaplutādiṣu
prākṛtasya dhvaneḥ kālaḥ śabdasyetyupacaryate

Sum : With regard to the short, long and prolated vowels-since a speech-unit (a vowel) is timeless and therefore fundamentally different, – it is the time of the primary sound which is metaphorically considered as belonging to the speech-unit.

Com : Prakṛti means the root. The sound that has come out from Prakṛti is called Prākṛtadhvani. Such a sound is born out of something (janya) and therefore time can create change in it. So that the Prākṛtadhvani has got the differenciation caused by one second, and two seconds. (ekamātra, dvimātra etc.). The same Prākṛtadhvani is the cause in the manifestation of Sphoṭaśabda. Prākṛtadhvani and Sphoṭaśabda are mixed like milk and water. It is impossible to separate them. Since both are inseparably mixed, the qualities of the Dhvani are reflected in Sphoṭaśabda. It is due to the Dhvani only that the Sphoṭaśabda appears in the form of ka-ga etc.

Notes : The form of Prākṛtadhvani itself looks like the form of Sphoṭaśabda. It is due to the hypothetical attribution (āropa) that we notice the difference caused by time as ekamātra, dvimātra and trimātra in a Sphoṭaśabda. That is how the Sphoṭaśabda differs. The short, long and prolated vowels are differnt from each other. That 'swhy, when followed by 't', the short vowel (like 'at') does not include the rest. The same is called 'taparakaraṇām'. Pāṇini instituted a Sūtra – 'Taparastatkālasya (Pāṇini 1-1-70)' for this purpose.

Thus the qualities of Prākrtadhvani are hypothetically attributed to Sphoṭaśabda. In truth, these differences are not there in Sphoṭa. Therefore, it is eternal.

Intro : As in the case of vowels, the difference of Vṛttis, viz. Druta, Madhya and Vilambita, must also be noticed in Sphoṭaśabda, as in both the cases *it is the time which causes the difference* – the author clarifies the doubt –

शब्दस्योर्ध्वमभिव्यक्तेः वृत्तिभेदे तु वैकृताः ।
ध्वनयः समुपोहन्ते स्फोटात्मा तैर्न भिद्यते ।।

77. śabdasyordhvamabhivyakteḥ vṛttibhede tu vaikṛtāḥ
dhvanayaḥ samupohante sphoṭātmā tairna bhidyate

Sum : It is, however, after the Śabda has been revealed (by the primary sounds) that the modified sounds are presented to the mind as distinctions of diction. The self of the Śabda is not devided into parts by them.

Com : Vikṛti means the external. The sounds produced through Vikṛti are called Vaikṛtadhvanis. Vaikṛtadhvanis keep on ringing the recollected Sphoṭaśabda, which is manifested by Prākṛtadhvanis, for sometime. Through this, the Vṛttis are taking place. One has to recite in Druta, talk in Madhya and teach/explain in Vilambita.

Therefore, since Vaikṛtadhvanis are useful to keep on ringing the Sphoṭaśabda in the ears for sometime, they cannot cause any difference in the Sphoṭaśabda.

So, as the Vṛtti cannot cause any difference, it will be the same 'akāra' in all the Vṛttis. On the other hand, the Pāṇinisūtra, where there is an 'akāra' pronounced in a particular Vṛtti, would have not been applicable in an example where the 'akāra' in another Vṛtti exists.

Notes : Dhvanis are of two types-Prākṛta and Vaikṛta. Before the manifestation of Śabda (Sphoṭa) there are Prākṛtadhvanis. They cause the Sphoṭaśabda obtain plurality and the difference of mātras. Vaikṛtadhvanis are those which take place after the Sphoṭaśabda is exhibited. They keep the sphoṭa for sometime. The same are called Vṛttis (Druta etc.). These Vaikṛtadhvanis won't cause the Sphoṭa to differ.

Intr : Untill now the author has substantiated that Dhvanis manifest the Sphoṭaśabda and such a Śabda is expressive. Now he answers two questions – *how the Dhvanis* manifest the Sphoṭaśabda and *what is manifestation ?*

इन्द्रियस्यैव संस्कारः शब्दस्यैवोभयस्य वा ।
क्रियते ध्वनिभिर्वादास्त्रयोऽभिव्यक्तिवादिनाम् ।।

78. indriyasyaiva saṃskāraḥ śabdasyaivobhayasya vā
kriyate dhvanibhirvādāstrayo'bhivyaktivādinām

Sum : There are three views among those who held the theory that Śabdas are manifested – 1. The sounds act upon the sense – organ, 2. The sounds act upon the Śabda, 3. The sounds act upon both.

Com : There are three groups among the supporters of manifestation –

1. The Dhvanis exercise Saṃskāra (refine) on the ear, and such an ear grasps the Śabda. 2. The Dhvanis refine the Śabda itself and such a Śabda is grasped by the ear. 3. The Dhvanis refine both the Śabda and the sense-organ and such an ear grasps the Śabda.

Notes : The ear grasps the Śabda. The Dhvanis provide with some sort of capacity to the ear which lacks the power to grasp. In case the ear has got the capacity to grasp the Dhvanis make the Śabda clear. This is called Saṃskāra (refinement). Then the ear would be capable of grasping.

All these arguments are related to Prākṛtadhvanis as they are the candidate, which suggest the Sphoṭaśabda.

Intro : The first half of the verse elaborates the first theory that the (Prākṛta) *Dhvanis refine the sense-organ*, whereas the latter half deals with the second theory that the *Dhvanis refine the* Śabda itself–

> इन्द्रियस्यैव संस्कारः समाधानाजजनादिभिः ।
> विषयस्य तु संस्कारः तद्गन्धप्रतिपत्तये ।।

79. indriyasyaiva samskāraḥ samādhānāñjanādibhiḥ
    viṣayasya tu samskāraḥ tadgandhapratipattaye

Sum : The first theory–concentration and application of ointment are acts upon the sense-organ (eye). The second theory-water is poured upon dried earth so that its smell can be felt.

Com : The Dhvanis refine the sense-organ itself. When he wishes to see the things far away, a yogi attains concentration. Through that the eye would get some capacity. Such an eye can perceive things that are far away. Some people see such far away things by application of specific ointment. We, when, due to age, loose sight, use spectacles for normal vision. All these examples are in support of the first theory, i.e. the refinement is to the eyes.

Similarly the Prākṛtadhvanis too would be helpful in providing ears with capacity that makes the sense organs grasp Śabdas. Then the ears grasp the Śabdas. Thus the Dhvani manifests the Śabda that is grasped by ears.

Here the word 'ādi' denotes spectacles etc. The purport of the theory is that the Śabda to be grasped needs no refinement.

On the other hand, the smell of scorched earth is known through adding water to it and that of the oil by keeping it in sunlight. It means that through the refinement with water and sunlight the smell of earth and oil can be felt. Here 'gandha' means smell (odour) that we generally feel (both good and bad). Nose is the sense-organ that grasps smell. Here the sense-organ is not refined. Refinement is done to the thing which is the base of the smell.

Similarly, due to the relation with dhvani, the Śabda itself is refined and it becomes the subject of the ears. It was due to the relation with dhvani, that the internal Śabda takes the form of external Śabda, which can be grasped.

Intro : Both, the sense-organ as well as the Śabda get the refinement-elaborates the author (*third theory*)–

> चक्षुषः प्राप्यकारित्वे तेजसा तु द्वयोरपि ।
> विषयेन्द्रिययोरिष्टः संस्कारः स क्रमो ध्वनेः ।।

80. cakṣuṣaḥ prāpyakāritve tejasā tu dvayorapi
    viṣayendriyayoriṣṭaḥ samskāraḥ sa kramo dhvaneḥ

Sum : According to the third theory - when the eye effects the reception of a thing, it is clear that both the object and the sense-organ are acted upon by the light and speech sounds operate in the same form.

Com : We perceive pot, cloth etc. in the dark with the help of light. There is no controversy in the thesis that light refines the things. On the other hand, according to the thesis that-the sense-organ is fixed and it perceives the things-the refinement is only to the thing. The other thesis-that the eye is in the form of rays, it travels everywhere, so that it reaches the object and grasps it – holds that the light refines the sense-organ too. The former thesis is floated by Bauddhas, whereas the latter by Naiyāyikas. The theory acceptable to Naiyāyikas, i.e., the Prākṛtadhvanis refine both the sense-organ (ear) as well as the Śabda, is elaborated in this verse. Even, Mīmāmsakas, who do not accept Sphoṭa but support the eternity of Śabda, referred to these three theories.

Intro : The author details the *three theories regarding the Prā*kṛta-dhvanis, that manifest the Sphoṭa –

स्फोटरूपविभागेन ध्वनेर्ग्रहणमिष्यते ।
कैश्चिद् ध्वनिरसंवेद्यः स्वतन्त्रोऽन्यैः प्रकल्पितः ।।

81. sphoṭarūpāvibhāgena dhvanergrahaṇamiṣyate
kaiścid dhvanirasamvedyaḥ svatantrónyaiḥ prakalpitaḥ

Sum : Certain theorists maintain that reception of the sound takes place without any seperation of it from the form of the Śabda, i.e, Sphota. Others, hold that sound is not perceptible. According to yet others, it is an independent manifesting agent.

Com : The light from the Sun illuminates the things like the pole. The light here is not perceived separately from the object-as this is the pole and this is the light.

Similarly, the Dhvanis, born out of the movement of the tongue, lips etc. do manifest the Sphoṭaśabda. The Dhvanis here are not considered different from the Śabda.

Even without their form being known to us, the sense-organs grasp the objects. In the same manner, the Dhvanis also, without our knowledge, manifest the Śabda.

After having lost our teeth, although we speak clearly, it is the Dhvani only that is conceived. Even when several people who have all the teeth intact speak at a time then also that are the Dhvanis which are heard. Therefore, eventhough it is mixed with Śabda, only the Dhvanis are known. The cries of birds and animals are heard and they have got no phonemes.

Intro : There are four Dhvanis in the word 'ghaṭaḥ'. All of them cannot manifest the Śabda simaltaneously. Then how is it possible that 'Dhvanis manifest the

Śabda' ?- while going to answer this question in the verse 83, *the author draws analogy* in verse 82 – यथानुवाकः श्लोको वा सोढत्वमुपगच्छति ।
आवृत्या, न तु स ग्रन्थः प्रत्यावृत्ति निरूप्यते ।।
प्रत्ययैरनुपाख्येयैः ग्रहणानुगुणैस्तथा ।
ध्वनिप्रकाशिते शब्दे स्वरूपमवधार्यते ।।

82. yathānuvākaḥ śloko va soḍhatvamupagacchati
āvṛtyā, na tu sa granthaḥ pratyāvṛtti nirūpyate
83. pratyayairanupākheyaiḥ grahanānuguṇaistathā
dhvaniprakāśite śabde svarūpamavadhāryate

Sum : Just as a chapter of hymns or a verse is apprehended by reciting ten times, but the same is not apprehended in each of the nine recitations, – the form of sequence-less Sphoṭa, which is revealed by the sounds through the agency of causal factors, which are appropriate to the cognition of Sphoṭa, but which are difficult to express distinctly (i.e. the hearer is not aware of the sense-data).

Com : One recites an anuvāka of Veda or a verse at his guru. He can commit it to memory after reciting ten times. Unless and until he recited it for the tenth time he could not get it by heart, i.e. by the last recitation he could hold it. Then the doubt arises as to whether the first nine recitations are in vain. But, since he recited so many times he could get it by the tenth time. It is illegitimate to argue that the earlier nine recitations are mere waste since he could not get it, as the exercise was much helpful in the end in getting it by heart.

Dhvanis manifest the Sphoṭa. There are ten dhvanis in the sentence 'ghaṭamānaya' (fetch the pot). The Sphoṭa can be suggested even by a single dhvani. This is like reciting for the first time. That much will not suffice to render a clear Śabda.

The Sphoṭaśabda is manifested by the earlier nine dhvanis, 'gh' 'a' etc. and made clear by the last dhvani, 'a'. As already explained the earlier nine dhvanis are not in vain, rather they assist the tenth dhvani in the manifestation of Sphoṭa.

So much so that like the anuvāka or verse, which is committed to memory by ten recitations, the Sphoṭa-śabda, which is manifested by ten dhvanis can express the meaning. For each time, the Śabda is manifested by each recitation, but, that cannot be considered as the fulfillment.

Therefore the cognition of last phoneme, supported by the impressions of the preceding phonemes is the cause in grasping the Śabda.

Intro : The idea expressed in the verse 83 *is being elaborated* –

नादैराहितबीजायामन्त्येन ध्वनिना सह।
आवृत्तपरिपाकायां बुद्धौ शब्दोऽवधार्यते।।

84. nādairāhitabījāyāmantyena, dhvaninā saha
āvṛttaparipākāyāṃbuddhau śabdóvadhāryate

Sum : Simultaneously with the last sound, the Śabda is aprehended by the mind in which the seed has been sown by the physical sounds, and in which ripening (or maturity of speech) has been brought about.

Com : Here 'BIJA' means samskāra (impression). 'PARIPĀKA' means a kind of Śakti (power or capacity) which will be useful in effecting the present action.

An impression is generated in the mind by the previous Dhvanis. Such a Samskāra would be capable of manifesting the Shoṭaśabda. The Sphoṭaśabda is manifested alongwith the last Dhvani. In the process the previous Dhvanis help in the form of impression.

Intro : In case the Dhvanis seperately manifest the Sphoṭaśabda, it can be concluded that there are neither any parts in a phoneme nor any phonemes in a word, nor any words in a sentence, since they don't have any suggesting things. *Nevertheless, phonemes, words and sentences do exist and how can this be possible* ?-the author answers this question –

असतश्चान्तराले यान् शब्दानस्तीति मन्यते।
प्रतिपत्तुरशक्तिः सा ग्रहणोपाय एव सः ।।

85. asataścāntarāle yān śabdānastīti manyate
pratipatturaśaktiḥ sā grahaṇopāya eva saḥ

Sum : So far as the non-existant forms, which a hearer considers as existing in the interval (i.e. between the utterance of the Śabda and revealing of Sphoṭa by them) are concerned, that is merely the incapacity on the part of the hearer; they are, in fact, only a means to the apprehension (of the complete Śabda, i.e. Sphoṭa).

Com : The Sphoṭaśabda is manifested through Dhvani either in the form of phoneme or word. The Sphoṭa is a single unit, it has no parts. There are no parts in a phoneme, nor any phonemes in a word, nor any words in a sentence. The feeling that they do exist is an illusion. They do not exist for those who can grasp the Sphoṭa through Dhvanis. In the above manner some people think that the Śabdas, which do not exist, in truth, do exist. They are incapable of grasping the Śabda (Sphoṭa). Only such people think so.

On the other hand, such Śabdas, thought to be existing, would be helpful for those incapable of grasping the Sphoṭaśabda. The conclusion is that the Śabda is akhanṇa (partless).

Intro : The author illustrates the following concept - In truth the Sphoṭaśabda has got no sequence. The sequence is there in the Dhvanis, which manifest the

Sphoṭa. Such a Śabda only is helping in the expression of meaning. *Otherwise, the Śabda cannot be grasped, nor is it capable of conveying the meaning–*

भेदानुकरणे ज्ञानस्य वाचश्चोपपल्वो ध्रुवः ।
क्रमोपसृष्टरूपा वाग ज्ञानं ज्ञेयव्यपाश्रयम् ।।

86. bhedānukaraṇe jñānasya vācaścopaplavo dhruvaḥ
kramopasṛṣṭarūpā vāk jñānam jñeyavyapāśrayam

Sum : There is semblence of distinctions in cognition; the attribution of distinctions of Śabdas is always seen. The word appears to be produced in sequence and cognition seems to be dependent on the cognised.

Com : In truth, the Sphoṭaśabda is partless and has got no sequence whatsoever. Since they are generators, the suggesting sounds (Vaikharydhvanis) consist of some parts and have got sequence. The qualities of the Dhvanis are imposed on Sphoṭaśabda. Knowledge is offered as an example-in fact, knowledge is a single unit. There are no parts in it. But since the things to be known are different, the difference among such things is imposed in knowledge.

The sequence of the Dhvanis is attributed to the Sphoṭaśabda and such a Śabda is expressing the meaning. Otherwise we cannot grasp the Śabda nor it can express the meaning. Knowledge is given as an example. Only the knowledge, which is mixed up with things like pot and cloth, is fit for grasping. Otherwise the knowledge would be without resort and therefore cannot be transmitted.

Intro : In the verse 85 it is stated that the fabrication of words, phonemes etc. is only a device (in grasping the Sphoṭaśabda)-(grahaṇopāya eva saḥ) - the words. phonemes etc. are created and described as the parts of the Sphoṭaśabda, which is partless and hence indivisible. They are a device fabricated for grasping the Sphoṭaśabda. In this connection a doubt arises–

There is identity in the quality/virtue of both the things. The threads are useful in knowing the cloth. On the contrary, the words and phonemes are not the parts of the sentence. They are not related with each other. An identical thing is useful in the knowledge of an indentical thing. Then *how can the non-identical words and phonemes be considered to be a device in the knowledge of Sphoṭaś*abda ? - the author clarifies the doubt–

यथाद्यसख्याग्रहणम् उपायः प्रतिपत्तये ।
संख्यान्तराणां भेदेऽपि तथा शब्दान्तरश्रुतिः ।।

87. yathādyasamkhyāgrahaṇam upāyaḥ pratipattaye
samkhyāntarāṇām bhedépi tathā śabdāntaraśrutiḥ

Sum : Just as earlier numbers (in a series) should be apprehended for the apprehension of subsequent ones, although the latter are different form the former, so is the apprehension of parts in a unit of speech i.e. an aid to the apprehension of the whole, Akhaṇḍavākyasphoṭa).

Com : Both the phonemes as well as the words are illusory and absolutely non-identical. Nevertheless, they can manifest the Sphoṭaśabda. In this context a number is offered as an example the first figure denotes 'ekatva' in a large number. The same is useful in counting of the rest of the digits as-two, three etc. of the same large number. The rest of the digits are not identical with the first digit. In a ten-digited number, the tenth digit is counted as ten. After the counting of all the digits as one, one etc. the last 'one' is ten. The same is the case in the present context also.

Intro : The dhvanis may have caused the knowledge of Śabda. But, *since the dhvanis are non-identical how can they manifest their form in the Śabda* ? Smoke suggests the existence of fire, but not by manifesting the form in it - the author clarifies the doubt–

प्रत्येकं व्यंजका भिन्ना वर्णवाक्यपदेषु ये
तेषामत्यन्तभेदेपि संकीर्णा इव शक्तयः ।।

88. pratyekam vyañjakā bhinnā varṇavākyapadeṣu ye
tesāmatyantabhedépi samkīrṇā iva śaktayaḥ

Sum : When in reality, revealing units in the phoneme, word and sentence function independently of each other, they appear to function in combination, although they are entirely different. Their capacities seem to be complicated.

Com : The revealing dhvanis in phoneme, word and sentence are not identical. They are different from each other. They reveal the things seperately. Rather, it seems that there are words in a sentence and phonemes in a word. For example the sentence gām ānaya (fetch the cow) is there. So much so that, although the three factors– sentence, word and phoneme are different they appear to be complicated due to the above identity. Therefore it holds water when it is said that words and phonemes are there in a sentence although the sentence is indivisible.

Intro : Katva, gatva etc. and the sequence are the qualities of Dhvani. Such qualities are not there in Sphoṭa. Then, since such a difference exists, how is it possible that such qualities appear in a Śabda ?-before answering this question in verse 90, *the author offers an example* in the first verse–

यथैव दर्शनैः पूर्वैः दूरात्सतमसेऽपि वा ।
अन्यथाकृत्य विषयमन्यथैवाध्यवस्यति ।।
व्यज्यमाने तथा वाक्ये वाक्याभिव्यक्तिहेतुभिः ।
भागावग्रहरूपेण पूर्वं बुद्धिः प्रवर्तते ।।

89. yathaiva darśanaiḥ pūrvaiḥ dūrātsantamasépi vā
anyathākṛtya viṣayamanyathaivādhyavasyati
90. vyajyamāne tathā vākye vākyābhivyaktihetubhiḥ
bhāgāvagraharūpeṇa pūrvam buddhiḥ pravartate

Sum : Just as on looking from a distance or in dark, one, at first misunderstands an object, and later on understands it otherwise (i.e. in its true structure). Likewise, during the manifestation of the sentence by its causes (viz. the smaller units like phonemes and words), the mind first functions as comprehending agent of component units (as real units).

Com : When the earlier dhvanis are emanated then that was phonemes and words which are felt and not the Akhaṇḍavākyasphoṭaśabda. Rather, the Sphoṭaśabda itself is felt not in its real form but in the unreal form of phonemes and words. It was through the last dhvani that the form of phonemes and words is gone and the real Vākyasphoṭa is manifested. Two examples are offered in this regard - even in broad daylihgt a man mistakes a tree, which is far away, for an elephant. Although it is nearby, in darkness one mistakes a zigzag rope for a serpant. Both were his first experiences. If the same man, being at the same place, thinks carefully then he concludes that both the things are tree and rope. Owing to some defect, first the real thing was thought to be somethingelse and the defect having gone, the same thing is identified as somethingelse, i.e., having given up the illusive form, the man identifies the real shape. The same process applies in the present context also.

The Vaiyākaraṇas believe that the phonemes and words are artificial. In fact they do not exist. Sentence is the real unit. The same is Sphoṭaśabda.

As it is described since the Padadhvanis are complicated, due to semblance, the mind functions in the form of phoneme-sounds and word-sounds. The real sentence remains after the illusion of the above said sounds is wiped out.

For example, before the sentence - 'Ghaṭamānaya' (fetch the pot) is manifested, the phonemes like gh etc. and the two words there are comprehended. It was due to the last sound that both the above said forms are manifested in the form of a sentence. The first experience was an illusion and the latter was the reality.

Intro : Someone looks at a distinct tree and cherishes an illusion that it is an elephant, it is not the same case with somebodyelse. He may think it to be a small hill-so that the illusive knowledge has got no consistency. Whereas in the case of sentence, if it is argued that it is indivisible and the phonemes and words are nothing but created artificially, there is consistency that there are at first the phonemes and next the words. So much so that the *illusion here has got no inconsistency. How is it possible* ?

The author answers the question –

यथानुपूर्वीनियमो विकारे क्षीरबीजयोः ।
तथैव प्रतिपत्तॄणां नियतो बुद्धिषु क्रमः ।।

91. yathānupūrvīniyamo vikāre kṣīrabījayoḥ
tathaiva pratipattṛṇām niyatobuddhiṣu kramaḥ

Sum : Just as there is a fixed sequence (in the stages) of the tranformation of milk (in to curd) and the seed (into the tree), similarly there is a fixed sequence in the series of the hearer's perceptions (of the intervening words phrases etc.)

Com : The indivisible Vākyasphoṭaśabda is the very candidate. There are neither words nor phonemes in it. Nevertheless, in order to facilitate the manifestation of the 'prime Śabda' there is a consistent sequence - first the phonemes and next the words are comprehended, then at the end the sentence is manifested, but not the other way round, i.e., first the words and next the phonemes. The phonemes and words are no doubt created but they have got a sequence which is consistent. Two examples are offered in this connection- 1. Milk transforms into curd. First the milk hardens to some extent and after sometime it hardens more. 2. When a seed is sown it gradually develops into seedling, plant etc. and becomes a tree. In this process it is not possible even to the creator to change the stage. The same is the situation in the present context too.

Intro : The *followers of Pūrvamīmāmsā* system hold that the phonemes are eternal group of phonemes is a word and that of words is a sentence, there is neither a word nor a sentence that is different from phonemes. Bhartṛhari argues that even in their case, it must be accepted that the difference between words like ghaṭa and paṭa is based on the sequence of the suggestive sounds –

भागवत्स्वपि तेष्वेव रूपभेदो ध्वनेः क्रमात् ।
निर्भागेष्वभ्युपायो वा भागभेदप्रकल्पनम् ।।

92. bhāgavatsvapi teṣveva rūpabhedo dhvaneḥ kramāt
nirbhāgeṣvabhyupāyo vā bhāgabhedaprakalpanam

Sum : And when they i.e. sentences words etc, are made up of real parts (granting the Mīmāmsakas' position), the difference in form (between two speech-units, for instance nadī-dīna) is really due to the (difference in the) sequece of their sounds. And where words, etc, are considered as not made up of (real) parts by the Akhaṇḍa-vādins), the fancying of parts is a means (to the realisation of the total unit).

Com : According to the theory of Mīmāmsakas the form of words like ghaṭaḥ and paṭaḥ has to be described in terms of the sequence of the sounds which are suggestive. Otherwise, the word manifested by each sound cannot be decided. The phonemes, for themselves, do not have any sequence. In case all the sounds are suggestive at a time since there are the same phonemes in both the words- nadī and dīna - it is not possible to differentiate between the two. Similarly, in the case of kapi-pika, rāja- jarā, yāma - māyā etc. too. Therefore, the sounds are suggestive. They are produced. They have a sequence. When the sequence is attributed to the suggested phonemes the difference among words is established. The point of view of Vaiyākaraṇas - the indivisible sentence is the real unit, phonemes and words are created - Grammarians hold it. In their case also the difference among phonemes and words is established depending on the sequence of sounds and through that the real Vākyasphoṭajñāna is achieved.

To sum up, the attribution of the natural sequence of sounds to the real Śabda is the same to both Mīmāmsakas and Vaiyākaraṇas.

The point to note is that Mīmāmsakas' theory holds that the contact of air is called sound whereas the Vaiyākaranas, take the phonemes like ka -ga etc. as sounds.

Intro : The author puts forth the view of those (Jātisphoṭavādins) who argue that the *Jāti* or general character, which is there in the Śabda, is the real *vā*caka (the expressing agent).

अनेकव्यक्त्यभिव्यङ्ग्या जातिः स्फोट इति स्मृता ।
कैश्चिद्व्यक्तय एवास्या ध्वनित्वेन प्रकल्पिता. ।।

93. anekavyaktyabhivyaṅgyā jātiḥ sphoṭa iti smṛtā
kaiścidvyaktaya evāsyā dhvanitvena prakalpitāḥ.

Sum : Some decided that the Śabdatvajāti, which is suggested by a number of varṇavyaktis, is the vācaka, these individual speech-sounds constitute the sound pattern of the word.

Com : Patañjali, the author of Mahābhāṣya, has analysed the Sphoṭaśabda as two, viz, Jātisphoṭa and Vyaktisphoṭa. Until now Bhartṛhari explained the Vyaktisphoṭa and now he goes on to Jātisphoṭa - Sphuṭati asmādarthaḥ (through this meaning is made clear) is the derivative meaning of the word Sphoṭa, i.e., Sphoṭa is the synonym of vācaka (the expressive śabda). Vyaktisphoṭa means Vyaktivācaka where as Jātisphoṭa means Jātivācaka.

Vyaktisphoṭavādin (the follower of Vyaktishphoṭa- theory) holds that the Sphoṭaśabda, manifested by dhvanis like ghaṭaḥ and paṭaḥ, is the vācaka.

The above said Śabdas refer to the jāti, i.e. ghaṭatva, paṭatva etc. which is there in those Śabdavyaktis. Several scholars have concluded that there is brevity in this theory. Then argues the Jātisphoṭavādin (follower of Jātisphoṭa-theory) that it is ghaṭatvajāti and not ghaṭaśabda which is vācaka. The Dhvanis in the form of phonemes can be suggestive of such a Jāti.

Note : Here Jāti does not mean the one proposed by Naiyāyikas (logicians), rather it refers to the Brahman, described in Vedānta system. This concept is clear in the author's words itself in Padakāṇḍa (Jātisamuddeśa).

Intro : The theory of Vyaktisphoṭavādin, that *only Śabdavyakti is the vā*caka - is being elaborated –

अविकारस्य शब्दस्य निमित्तैर्विकृतो ध्वनिः ।
उपलब्धौ निमित्तत्वमुपयाति प्रकाशवत् ।।

94. avikārasya śabdasya nimittairvikṛto dhvaniḥ
upalabdhau nimittatvamupayāti prakāśavat

Sum : Just as light reveals objects, the speech sounds produced by their causes become the cause of the immutable śabda.

Com : There is ghaṭatvajāti in a ghaṭa. Ghaṭa is a resort of such a Jāti. This is how the terms Jāti and Vyakti are generally applied.

Sphoṭaśabda is not like that. The Śabdavyakti is eternal. It is only one which pervades Ākāśa (space). There is no Jāti in it. The movement of sound producing organs effects difference in the sounds and not in Sphoṭaśabda. The Sphoṭavyakti is not born out of dhvani. Nevertheless, dhvani can suggest Sphoṭavyakti. Light is offered as an example to explain this concept - the light of a lamp does not generate things like ghaṭa. The things are not dependent on light. Nevertheless, it illuminates them the same is the case in the present context also.

As soon as one attains Brahmajñāna, the Jāti also perishes. So Jāti cannot withstand while the conclusions are drawn. Therefore, the Vyaktisphoṭa theory is tenable.

Intro : It is not appropriate to say that dhvanis are suggestive of the eternal Śabda as only non-eternal things like ghaṭa and paṭa are manifested by the light of the lamp. *How can eternal things be manifested ?* - the author clarifies the doubt –

न चानित्येष्वभिव्यक्तिः नियमेन व्यवस्थिता।
आश्रयैरपि नित्यानां जातीनां व्यक्तिरिष्यते।।

95. na cānityeṣvabhivyaktiḥ niyamena vyavasthitā
āśrayairapi nityānām jātīnām vyaktiriṣyate

Sum : Being revealed as not established is invariably pertaining to non-eternal things. Universals which are eternal are also considered to be revealed by those (i.e the particulars) in which they inhabit.

Com : The light of the lamp illuminates the things like 'ghaṭa'. The illuminated things are non-eternal. So that it is possible to rule that the illuminated things are non-eternal. In such a context, the Śabda should also be non-eternal, in case it is the presumed that the Spoṭaśabda is manifested through Dhvanis. But the above argument cannot be acceptable to the school of Grammarians. This verse offers a clarification to this doubt –

There is no any such regulation that manifestation is applicable only to eternal objects. the Śāstras hold that there are Jātis like ghaṭatva, paṭatva, gotva etc. in the Vyaktis, i.e. ghaṭa, paṭa, go etc. and the same are eternal. Also that such Jātis are illuminated by Vyaktis like ghaṭa.

That's why objects like ghaṭa etc. are called Vyaktis. Vyakti is that which manifests. People think that objects in such a form are ghaṭas and among all such things there is ghaṭatvajāti.

Therefore, since the Jātis are manifested by the Vyaktis they are resorted by, there won't be any impropriety in the manifestation of the eternal Spoṭaśabda by dhvanis. There is no any rule that only non-eternal things get manifested.

Intro : The relation of suggestive and suggested is experienced only in case of a lamp and nearby ghaṭa. A lamp at a faraway place cannot be able to illuminate the ghaṭa. In the present context, the dhvani, manifested by sound-producing-organs, is there in the mouth, whereas the Śabda is there in the mind. Then *how can it be possible to apply the relation of suggestive and suggested between dhvani and Śabda which are at different places* ? - the author answers the question –

देशादिभिश्च सम्बन्धो दृष्टः कायवतामिह।
देशभेदविकल्पेऽपि न भेदो ध्वनिशब्दयोः।।

96. deśādibhiścha sambandho dṛṣṭaḥ kāyavatāmiha
deśabhedavikalpépi na bhedo dhvaniśabdayoḥ

Sum : In day to day life (only) concrete objects are found to have relation with place and the like (time etc). And even accepting the alternative (that difference in place, etc. applies also to those that are not concrete objects) there is no such difference between the speech-sound and the Śabda (it reveals).

Com : The term 'place' is applicable oniy in the case of tangible (concrete) things. Things like ghaṭa and gauḥ are tangible and hence they have connection with place and time. Śabda is not so. It is pervasive in nature. It is spread allover (the space). Therefore the connection of place which is seen in the case of those with their sides limited, is not applicable to the pervasive Śabda.

In common parlance, sentences like-he is speaking in the house, he is speaking on the road etc. are employed and through this it appears that the Śabda has got the difference of place. But such a difference is only created and not genuine. A non-concrete or non-tangible thing such as Śabda cannot have the connection of place, whatsoever.

Note : In the first line 'ca' means 'eva' (only). 'kāyavatāmapi' is the version in another text.

Intro : A single thing being illuminated may have many illuminators. A ghaṭa can be illuminated by a lamp, sunlight and the light of a gem. There is no any such rule that only one among the said things can be capable of illuminating. Such is the context of the revealed and the revealer or suggested and suggestive. In the present context Śabda is the illuminated thing. Dhvanis are illuminators. The Śabda cannot be revealed by anything other than dhvanis. So much so that *the relation between a Śabda and dhvanis is that of generated and generative and not suggested and suggestive* - Bhartṛhari answers the question –

ग्रहणग्राह्ययोः सिद्धा नियता योग्यता यथा ।
व्यङ्ग्यव्यञ्जकभावेन तथैव स्फोटनादयोः ।।

97. grahaṇagrāhyayoḥ siddhā niyatā yogyatā yathā
vyaṅgyavyañjakabhāvena tathaiva sphoṭanādayoḥ

Sum : Just as there exists an invariable competence of the revealed and the revealer between a perceiving sense - organ and the thing it perceives, so does it exist between the Śabda and the speech - sounds.

Com : The perceiving sense - organ in the eye (it is believed that the sense-organs are minute and they cause the results such as reflection etc.) manifests the perceived object, such as ghaṭa. Neither some other quality, nor another sense-organ in the other part are capable of manifesting the form of ghaṭa. Therefore, the sense-organ in the eye only is considered as the suggestive. The relation between the eye (sense-organ) and the object is invariable. The same relation is called yogyatā (capability). But the above two things do not have the relation of generated and generative. The form of Ghaṭa and/or ghaṭa are not born out of the eye i.e. the sense-organ. Similarly, the dhvanis can manifest an invariable Śabda. Such a capacity of dhvanis is invariable. The same is yogyatā. (See Padakāṇḍa - Sambandha-Samuddeśa - 29)

Intro : Another answer is offered by the author to the same question –

सदृशग्रहणानां च गन्धादीनां प्रकाशकम् ।
निमित्तं नियतं लोके प्रतिद्रव्यमवस्थितम् ।।

98. sadṛśagrahaṇānam ca gandhādīnām prakāśakam
nimittam niyatam loke pratidravyamavasthitam

Sum : And it is observed (through our experience) that, in the case of (various) smells and the like which are perceived by the same sense-organ, there is a separate causal factor for each substance.

Com : The manifesting thing may vary in case there is dissimilarity between the perceived and perceiver. There is dravyatva in the suggested ghaṭa and guṇatva in the perceiver, i.e. the eye (sense-organ). Since both these things are dissimilar, the manifesting thing may be variable. The form of the sense-organ (eye) would be the cause of manifestation of the form of ghaṭa, nothing else. In the present context, since there is similarity between the suggestive dhvanis and suggested Śabda, there is no any regulation that the suggestive should be variable. Similarly, if the smell of the soil is to be perceived then the smell of the sense-organ, i.e. nose, would be suggestive of it. Here, since both are similar, the suggesting thing is invariable.

Intro : The Prākṛtadhvanis illuminate the Sphoṭaśabda. The Sphoṭa is eternal. It is invariable. Therefore, Vaiyākaraṇas hold that the Sphoṭa is suggested or vyaṅgya. Rather, such an argument appears to be contrary to the (worldly) day to day experience. We cannot perceive ghaṭa etc. in darkness. We use a lamp to see them. Then the darkness is gone and the things, ghaṭa etc. are seen. It is obvious here that the lamp is (suggestive) illuminative and ghaṭa etc. are (suggested) illuminated. The smallness or the largeness of the illuminative lamp is not reflected in the illuminated ghaṭa - in case the lamp is small the ghaṭa will not be small or in case the lamp is large the ghaṭa will not be large. Similarlly, in case ten lamps illuminate the ghaṭa there won't be ten ghaṭas. This is the position of illuminative and illuminated (or suggestive and suggested). To sum up, the illuminated thing does not change/vary in relation with the illuminative. It will be in it's real form. In the present context, the case does not look to be the same. In relation with the suggestive dhvanis the Sphoṭaśabda is seen to be increasing and decreasing. Similary, in case the suggestive dhvanis are so many the Sphoṭa, i.e. the suggested (or Vyaṅgya) is also seen as many, like ghaṭa, paṭa etc.. Therefore, the qualities of the suggestive sounds are seen in the Sphoṭaśabda. The same is not the case in day to day experience, it is rather different. So much so that it is legitimate to say that the Sphoṭaśabda is generated. Then *how can it be possible to hold that the Śabda is eternal?* the author answers the question –

प्रकाशकानां भेदांश्च प्रकाश्योऽर्थोऽनुवर्तते ।
तैलोदकादिभेदे तत्प्रत्यक्षं प्रतिबिम्बके ।।

99. prakāśakānām bhedāmśca prakāśyórthónuvartate
tailodakādibhede tatpratyakṣam pratibimbake

Sum : The object revealed (refleted) partakes of the attributes of the reflecting medium. This is obvious in different kinds of reflections (of an object) produced in oil, water and the like (so much so that the attributes of the speech-sounds revealing the word are transferred to the word).

Com : There are occasions where we find reflection of the qualities of the illuminative in the illuminated. The face will be black in case it reflected in oil, clear in a mirror, larger in a magnifying lense, unclear in an unclear mirror and vertical in a sword.

Notes : A single image of Sun is seen in great number in case it reflects in water that is in different places. The single caitanya (or consciousness) is seen differently due to the difference in antaḥkaraṇa (individual soul). A mammoth elephant will have a small reflection in a small mirror. Therefore, it cannot be ruled out that the qualities of suggestive won't reflect in the suggested.

So, it is possible that a single Spoṭaśabda may be manifested in so many forms due to the plurality of the suggestive dhvanis. In truth Sphoṭaśabda is not generated.

Intro : It can be held that the form of the face etc. generated afresh in substances like oil, diamond, mirror etc. and not reflected. Then, *the above offered examples are not competent* in substantiating the claim that the qualities of suggestive thing would reflect in the suggested - Bhartṛhari clarifies –

विरुद्धपरिमाणेषु वज्रादर्शतलादिषु ।
पर्वतादिसरूपाणां भावानां नास्ति सम्भवः ।।

100. viruddhaparimāṇeṣu vajrādarśatalādiṣu
parvatādisarūpāṇām bhāvānām nāsti sambhavaḥ

Sum : And surely, concrete objects of the type of mountains cannot have existence (except as their reflections) in diamonds, mirror-surface and the like of incompatible size.

Com : On the suface of diamond etc. objects like mountain and elephant do reflect and no new thing is produced. It is impossible. The objects, i.e., mountain etc., have got a mammoth size and then how can the reflections of such things with same size, take place afresh in small things like diamond, mirror etc. ? Therefore, the example offered in verse 99 is genuine.

Intro : The author *concludes the statement* in verse 49, i.e. the difference in Sphoṭaśabda is due to the difference in suggestive dhvanis –

तस्मादभिन्नकालेषु वर्णवाक्यपदादिषु।
वृत्तिकालः स्वकालश्च नादभेदाद्विभाव्यते।।

101. tasmādabhinnakāleṣu varṇavākyapadādiṣu
vṛttikālaḥ svakālaśca nādabhedādvibhāvyate

Sum : Therefore, the period of the speechsounds and of Vṛtti (drutamadhya-vilambitas) are assigned to the phoneme, sentence, word etc. (discourse), which are themselves without time-distinctions.

Com : Since Sphoṭaśabda is eternal, the qualities of time won't/cannot create any distinctions in it. It is manifested by the dhvanis. The qualities of dhvanis reflect in Sphoṭaśabda. Prākṛtadhvanis manifest the Sphoṭa. Since the Śabda is mixed with them it attains the time-distinctions, i.e. ekamātra etc.. Since Vaikṛtadhvanis are external their qualities won't reflect in Sphoṭa. Rather, they can cause the existence of Sphoṭa for some time.

Like thus the Prākṛtadhvanis cause ekamātra etc. difference (of time) in Sphoṭa, whereas Vaikṛtadhvanis cause the time distinctions i.e. druta etc. in Sphoṭa.

Intro : The Vaiyākaraṇas have accepted two theories (quite opposite)-Śabda is eternal and Śabda is non-eternal. They however hold that the former is important and genuine theory and right from verse 44 till 102, the author, in accordance with the same, has explicated the Sphoṭaśabda, the suggestive dhvanis that cause it, the relation of suggestive and suggested etc.. This theory is meant for intellectuals (uttamādhikārins).

In order to make the Śāstra available to those who are not quite intelligent (madhyamādhikārins) the Vaiyākaraṇas have resorted to the second theory, widely known as 'Kāryaśabdavāda'. According to this theory 'the Śabda is produced' like any other object i.e., ghaṭa, paṭa etc. The *author explains the Sphoṭaśabda* and *Dhvani verse* 102 118, *in terms of Kāryaśabdavāda* –

यस्संयोगविभागाभ्यां करणैरुपजन्यते।
स स्फोटः शब्दजाः शब्दा ध्वनयोऽन्यैरुदाहृताः।।

102. yassamyogavibhāgābhyām karaṇairupajanyate
sa sphoṭaḥ śabdajāḥ śabdā dhvanayonyairudāhṛtāḥ

Sum : The propegators of another school say that the Sphoṭa is that which is produced by the union and disunion of speech-organs and dhvanis are sounds born from this Sphoṭa.

Com : The air travels (inside) and touches the organs like throat, palate, lips etc. and causes the production of phonemes like-a, i, ka etc.. These are the candidates of expressing meaning, called Vācakas and the same are also called Sphoṭaśabda. These are the things born first.

Some other Śabdas are born out of this Sphoṭaśabda. They are called Dhvanis (sounds). The Prākṛtadhvanis, which are suggestive of Sphoṭaśabda in Nityaśabdavāda (the theory which holds that the Śabda is eternal), are considered as Sphoṭaśabda in Kāryaśabdavāda and the Vaikṛtadhvanis are taken as Dhvanis. Firstly, the Sphoṭaśabda is born at organs like palate etc.. From that another type of sounds are born. They are the dhvanis.

Intro : Firstly the expressive Śabda is generated at throat, palate etc.. The same is called Sphoṭaśabda. Another type of sounds are produced from that Śabda - it is proposed in verse 102. The author *analyses the process –*

अल्पे महति वा शब्दे स्फोटकालो न भिद्यते।

परस्तु शब्दसंतानः प्रचयापचयात्मकः ।।

103. alpe mahati vā śabde sphoṭakālo na bhidyate

parastu śabdasantānaḥ pracayāpacayātmakaḥ

Sum : Whether the speech-sound is short or long, the measure of the Śabda does not change. The subsequent sound (i.e., the modified speech sound) which arises out of the primary speech-sounds, is expanded or contracted in its form.

Com : Since Śabda has got no concrete form it cannot have qualifiers like short and long. Rather the sounds that have come out of the Sphoṭaśabda will get such expressions like short and long. These terms are attributed to the Sphoṭaśabda also. Therefore, like a needle and mountain, the Śabda, which has got the superimposed smallness and largeness, also spreads through small and large place.

Intro : In verse 102 it is stated that the Sphoṭaśabda is produced first and then the dhvanis from that. Now the author gives *another theory* which holds that the Sphoṭaśabda is produced alongwith the dhvanis –

दूरात्प्रभेव दीपस्य ध्वनिमात्रं तु लक्ष्यते।

घण्टादीनां च शब्देषु व्यक्तो भेदः स दृश्यते।।

104. dūrātprabheva dīpasya dhvanimātram tu lakṣyate

ghaṇṭādīnām ca śabdeṣu vyakto bhedaḥ sa dṛśyate

Sum : Another school is explained – the lamp does not move, so also the Sphoṭa; but the light is felt at a distance - so also the Nāda. (the primary sound is called Sphoṭa, whereas the modified sounds are called Nāda (Nāda-vibration).

Com : The lamp is born along with light. Similary, the Sphoṭaśabda is also born alongwith the dhvanis-i.e. both are born simultaneously. The lamp exists at the same point of place, but the light spreads to some distance. In the same manner Śabda is at the same place (where it is born) but the dhvanis are carried to some distance - the sound is felt at a distance, but not the Śabda. When ten people speak simultaneously the words are not audible, but the sound is felt.

Dhvanis are heard when a bell is rung-those are called Sphoṭaśabda. Some vibrations come out of the Śabda - they are dhavanis. The difference between Sphoṭa and Nāda is clearer in this example.

Notes : Each part of this verse offers an example. The ghaṇṭānāda example is useful in setting at rest the doubt that the dhvani is not felt seperately from the Sphoṭaśabda. Although it is difficult to differentiate, since both are produced simultaneously, the dhvani is clear when groups of people speak (simultaneously). The example of Dīpaprabhā is useful in substantiating the view that the dhvani, emanating from Sphoṭa, travells to faraway places. Both the thoeries explained in verses 102 & 104 are due to the difference of opinion among those who hold that the Śabda is non-eternal.

Intro : the author reasons the *existence of long and prolated sounds and the Vṛ*ttis (druta etc.) in terms of non-eternity of Śabda –

द्रव्याभिघातात्प्रचितौ भिन्नौ दीर्घप्लुतावपि ।
कम्पेतूपरते जाता नादा वृत्तेर्विशेषकाः ।।

105. dravyābhighātātpracitau bhinnau dīrghaplutāvapi
kampetūparate Jātā nādā vṛttervis̒eṣakāḥ

Sum : The long and prolated sounds which are different (from each other) are produced by the striking of the organs of speech. And the sounds which modify the Vṛtti (druta etc.) arise after the cessation of the movements (of the organs).

Com : The internal air comes up to the throat and makes the tip of the tongue touch the organs of speech. It has got a distinctive capacity. Due to the same, vibration takes place. Such vibration modifies in accordance with the phoneme. Therefore, the long and prolated sounds (dīrghas and plutas) are also different. Even after the swich is put off the fan does not stop at once. It runs for some more time. The vibrations are similar to that.

After the cessation of the vibrations the Vaikharydhvanis are born. They cause the Vṛttis - Druta, Madhya and Vilambita.

The Śabda is produced through the touch of air at speech-organs. Although there is no natural diversity, different virtues take place due to the vibrations. Thus the long and prolated sounds become distinct. After the cessation of vibrations the Vaikṛtadhvanis come into existence. They cannot cause any dissimilarity in Sphoṭaśabda. They cause the difference in Vṛtti.

Notes : Therefore the long sound in Vṛttis does not change. The verse is applicable to the other theory, i.e., Sphoṭaśabda is eternal.

Intro : It is stated in verse 105 that the Vaikṛtadhvanis come into existence as soon as the virbrations are subsided. Now the author refers to *another school*, which holds that even while the vibrations are there, the *Vaikṛtadhvanis* are formed out of *Sphoṭaśabda* –

अनवस्थितकम्पेऽपि करणे ध्वनयोऽपरे।
स्फोटादेवोपजायन्ते ज्वाला ज्वालान्तरादिव।।

106. anavasthitakampépi karaṇe dhvanayópare
sphoṭādevopajāyante jvālā jvālāntarādiva

Sum : Another school - even before the virbrations of the speech organs (which produce the Śabda) have subsided, other sounds, are formed from the Sphoṭa itself, as one flame from another.

Com : Flames are produced when the drysticks come in contact with fire. When more sticks are added to the flame more flames are formed. Similarly, vibrations take place due to the touch of air at speech-organs. While the vibrations are still there, the Vaikṛtadhvanis are formed out of Sphoṭaśabda.

Intro : The origin of *Śabda* in terms of Kāryaśabdavāda, is described, in accordance with different systems, *in eleven verses* –

वायोरणूनां ज्ञानस्य शब्दत्वापत्तिरिष्यते।
कैश्चिद्दर्शनभेदो हि प्रवादेष्वनवस्थितः।।

107. vāyoraṇūnām jñānasya śabdatvāpattiriṣyate
kaiściddarśanabhedo hi pravādeṣvanavasthitaḥ

Sum : According to Śikṣā-School Vāyu is the cause of Śabda. Jaina-school proposes atoms to be the cause and Patañjali says that consciousness becomes Śabda. There are different viewpoints of different schools in this matter.

Com : The followers of Śikṣāśāstra hold that air is the cause of Śabda, Jainas take it as atoms. Whereas Patañjali considers it to be the knowledge. It is difficult to confirm as to which is the cause of Śabda.

Intro : The theory of the founder of Śikṣāśāstra, i.e. air is the cause of Śabda is explained in two verses.

लब्धक्रियः प्रयत्नेन वक्तुरिच्छानुवर्तिना ।
स्थानेष्वभिहतो वायुः शब्दत्वं प्रतिपद्यते ।।

108. labdhakriyaḥ prayatnena vakturicchānuvartinā
sthānesvabhihato vāyuḥ śabdatvam pratipadyate

Sum : The Śikṣā-school is elaborated :

The air which is stirred by the speaker's effort following his desire to speak, strikes the speech centers and produces Śabda.

Com : When the speaker wishes to express his idea, certain process takes place-firstly the idea is formed in the mind. Then the desire for expression. After that the speaker makes an endeavour. Here endeavour means tightening the vocal chords opening the lips, stretching the jaws, the act of swallowing etc. Through this endeavour, the air at the navel moves, takes the idea, travels upto the throat through heart, touches the speech centers and takes the form of Śabda like a, i, u etc..

Intro : How the evolution of air which has got the virtue of *accumulation, into Śabdas* is possible ? -answers the author –

तस्य कारणसामर्थ्याद्वेगात् प्रचयधर्मणः ।
सन्निपाताद्विभज्यन्ते सारवत्योऽपि मूर्तयः ।।

109. tasya kāraṇasāmarthyādvegān pracayadharmaṇaḥ
sannipātādvibhajyante sāravatyópi mūrtayaḥ

Sum : Even solid & strong objects are broken by air which possesses the attributes of speed and accumulation, blowing with the capacity to cause (such breaking).

Com : The air has got two virtues, viz. speed and accumulation. Due to the specific endeavor of man, the speed of air is manifested and the air moves. Due to the speed only the air touches the speech organs, ceases its accumulating quality and eventually forms into different Śabdas. A mass of dry soil, breaks when it falls upon a stone. Similarly, the accumulated air, when falls at the speech centers, forms into different Śabdas.

Intro : The atom-theory of Jainas is being expounded by two verses –

अणवः सर्वशक्तित्वाद् भेदसंसर्गवृत्तयः ।
छायातपतमश्शब्दभावेन परिणामिनः ।।

110. aṇavaḥ sarvaśaktitvād bhedasamsargavṛttayaḥ
chāyātapatamaśśabdabhāvena pariṇāminaḥ

The atoms, which unite and seperate, transform themselves into shadows, light, darkness and the Śabda on account of their possessing all capacities (i.e. the capacity to be transformed into all things)

Com : Here in this verse the word 'aṇavaḥ' refers to the "tanmātrās" which are the very constituents of 'Mahābhūtas' and famous in Kapila-Sāmkhya-school. (and not the ones mentioned in Tarkaśāstra).

There are distinct qualities in 'tanmātrās' and due to that they can seperate and unite. Among the tanmātrās the blue atoms turn into shadow and dark, the white atom into sunlight and the Śabda atoms into solidified Śabdas. They posses the capacity of causing separation and uniting.

Intro : Since *the atoms in the form of Śabdatanmātrās* are eternal why won't they change in the form of magnified Śabda ? We do not experience such a thing ? - the author answers the question --

स्वशक्तौ व्यज्यमानायां प्रयत्नेन समीरिताः ।
अभ्राणीव प्रचीयन्ते शब्दाख्याः परमाणवः ।।

111. svaśaktau vyajyamānāyām prayatnena samīritāḥ
abhrāṇīva pracīyante śabdākhyāḥ paramāṇavaḥ

Sum : When their capacity is being revealed these atoms (tanmātrās) called Śabda, prompted by the effort (of the speaker) collect together like clouds (in the sky).

Com : Here effort means the movement effected by one's adṛṣṭa (nemesis). The prāṇavāyu (oxygen) accumulates the moving Śabda-tanmātrās. During rainy season the clouds, urged by the air, turn into water. The process, otherwise, is not possible.

Similary, the Śabdatanmātrās, spread alover, get the movement caused by nemesis, accumulated by the Prāṇavāyu, and appear in the form of magnified Śabdas. Without the above process they cannot change into sthūlaśabdas (magnified Śabdas).

Intro : Now the author explains *the theory of consciousness proposed by Patañjali in Mahābhāṣya under the sūtra 'ākhyātopayoge' (1-4-29) of Panini*, by four verses :–

अथायमान्तरो ज्ञाता सूक्ष्मवागात्मना स्थितः ।
व्यक्तये स्वस्य रूपस्य शब्दत्वेन विवर्तते ।।

112. athāyamāntaro jñātā sūkṣmavāgātmanā sthitaḥ
vyaktaye svasya rūpasya śabdatvena vivartate

Sum : The inner knower who exists in the subtle quintessential speech transforms himself into (audible) speech for the purpose of revealing his nature.
Com : In the beginning there was only the form of Śabda. It itself devides into speech and mind. The mind transforms into Vṛtti or expressive power. The transformation is knowledge. Since the mind is the resort of knowledge (in the form of Vṛtti) it is known as 'jñātā'. The initial picture is very minute. It does not have the form of katva, gatva etc.

Such a mind, when the need of expressing the idea within arises, transforms its minute form into a magnified Śabda. For this process the heat in the body is instrumental.
Note : The mind, through expressive power, attains the form of Śabda and the same is described as "manifestation of knowledge as Śabda". Since the user of Śabda has to transform his knowledge to others only through Śabda. it is considered that knowledge itself transforms into Śabda. Vaiyākaraṇas believe that Śabda has life.
Intro : The author explains the process of the *transformation of knowledge into magnified Śabda* –

स मनोभावमापद्य तेजसा पाकमागतः ।
वायुमाविशति प्राणमथासौ समुदीर्यते ।।

113. sa manobhāvamāpadya tejasā pākamāgataḥ
vāyumāviśati prāṇamathāsau samudīryate

Sum : The knower taking the form of the mind and ripening in the fire (of the stomach) enters the life-breath and it is then uttered.
Com : Jaṭhārāgni (digestive fire) and the heat in the nerves are referred to by the word 'tejasā', here. Both these cause ripening effect to knowledge, which is in the form of expressive power (of mind). Here 'Pāka' means causing the capacity of conceiving the matter to the 'jñātā', who is in the form of mind.

With such ripening only, the mind puts its form in the Prāṇa-vāyu (life-breath). Such a vāyu is instigated up to the throat by the capacity of life-power (jīvaśakti). The prāṇavāyu travels naturally. Instigation is the nature of life-power.
Notes : The outside air, due to lack of this process does not transform into Śabda, although it touches the speech-organs.
Intro : The *further process* is explained –

अन्तः करणतत्वस्य वायुराश्रयतां गतः ।
तद्धर्मेण समाविष्टः तेजसैव विवर्तते ।।

114. antaḥkaraṇatattvasya vāyurāśrayatām gataḥ
taddharmeṇa samāviṣṭastejasaiva vivartate

Sum : The breath which has become the substratum of the mental principle is suffused with the mind's attributes and manifested (after it passes) through the fire (of the stomach).

Com : The prāṇavāyu (or life-breath) is the substratum of mind. The mind cannot exist without that air. Such a mind mixes with the air, comes out with the help of digestive fire, and then again transforms into the form of mind. An example – fire is necessary for cooking. Fire resorts to wood. After some time it transforms into heat.

Note : Initially it is in the form of Śabda and later transforms into mind when it resorts to the air, and while coming out with the help of fire the mind in the form of Śabda is manifested.

Intro : Further, the process of *transformation of Prāṇavāyu*, which has got identity with mind, into phonemes is elaborated –

विभजन् स्वात्मनो ग्रन्थीन् श्रुतिरूपैः पृथग्विधैः ।
प्राणो वर्णानभिव्यज्य वर्णेष्वेवोपलीयते ।।

115. vibhajan svātmano granthīn śrutirūpaiḥ pṛthagvidhaiḥ
prāṇo varṇānabhivyajya varṇeṣvevopalīyate

Sum : Breaking up its inherent knots (i.e. its continuous current) the breath reveals the syllables through different and distinct speech-sounds and merges into the syllables themselves.

Com : The prāṇavāyu, through the phonemes coming out, expresses its knot-like parts, which object the manifestation of phonemes, in the form of phonemes and thus manifests the phonemes. After that the Vāyu will be in the form of phoneme and not Vāyu.

Notes : While coming out the Vāyu hits the speech-centers as well as itself and thus the manifestation of phonemes takes place.

Granthi means knot. As it is in the case of a rope, there are parts where the current of air is obstructed. Knots are there in the mind too. The same are hurdles in attaining the ātmatattvajñāna (or the knowledge of noumenon of soul)

Right from the verse 107, the way Śabda is produced is explained in accordance with all the three schools. The importance of Vāyu is common to all. Prānavāyu is primal. The difference in schools is due to the subordinates.

Intro : '*The entire universe* (not only Ākāśa) *is suffused with Śabda-argue some followers of Śikṣā* –

अजस्रवृत्तिः यः शब्दः सूक्ष्मत्वान्नोपलभ्यते।
व्यजनाद्वायुखि स स्वनिमित्तात्प्रतीयते।।

116. ajasravṛttiḥ yaḥ śabdaḥ sūkṣmatvānnopalabhyate
vivartamānā sthāneṣu saiṣā bhedam prapadyate

Sum : Śabda, though it is ever-existing, is not experienced because it is too subtle. It is realised through the approapriate causal factors just as air is through fanning.

Com : Śabda is pervasive. It appears in non-living things like pot etc. in the form of sound, in living things too-like birds etc. in the form of sound but in human beings in the form of both sound and phoneme. But the Śabda can be grasped only when it touches the speech-organs like lips. Then it is heard in the form of phoneme. When there is contact between a stick and drum then it is heard in the form of Sound (Dhvani). Without cause it cannot be relised. The reason is its sutleness. Vāyu is offered as an example- Vāyu pervades the universe. Nevertheless, we experience it through the skin, only at sometimes, not always. Although it is not experienced by skin there is air in minute form. The same is revealed through fan, and grasped by the skin.

To sum up, the Śabda which pervades the entire universe in minute form is experienced due to some cause or the other.

Intro : The view of *another school* regarding Śabda –

तस्य प्राणे च या शक्तिः या च बुद्धौ व्यवस्थिता।
विवर्तमाना स्थानेषु सैषा भेदं प्रपद्यते।

117. tasya prāṇe ca yā śaktiḥ yā ca buddhau vyavasthitā
vivartamānā sthāneṣū saiṣā bhedam prapadyate

Sum : The powers of speech resident in the breath and in the mind undergo transformation (into speech) at the centres of speech production and assume the distinctions (of revealed speech).

Com : Śabda is there in the mind (buddhi) in minute form. The minute form is refered to as 'Śakti'. The mind transforms the minute Śabda to Prāṇavāyu. Both these powers are produced in the speech organs and reveal distinct phonemes like a, i, ka etc.

The Śabda is there in the mind initially. The power in the mind is transformed to prāṇa. Both mix up and cause the manifested Śabda.

Notes : It was only due to the relation with the mind that prāṇavāyu touches appropriate speeech-organs in order to produce phonemes in accordance with the meaning desired to express. Otherwise, phonemes would have come out at random.

Without the relation of prāṇavāyu the mind cannot transform into Śabda. Therefore, initially there will be the minute Śabda in the mind. Due to its initiative only the minute Śabda comes to Prāṇavāyu. Both combinely touch the speech-centers and produce the phonemes.

Intro : 'Śabda is the sole cause of all the transactions in the world the author proposes by describing *the greatness of Śabda by 15 verses* –

शब्देष्वेवाश्रिता शक्तिः विश्वस्यास्य निबन्धिनी।
यन्नेत्रः प्रतिभात्माऽयं भेदरूपः प्रतीयते।।

118. śabdeṣvevāśritā śaktiḥ viśvasyasya nibandhinī
yannetraḥ pratibhātmāyam bhedarūpaḥ pratīyate

Sum : The power which is based on Śabdas is the cause of (all transactions) in this universe. The universe which has a single intuition (pratibhā) as its soul is perceived as manifold through the Śabda as the eye.

Com : Śabda is the sole cause of the gamut of transactions across the globe. The entire world is in the form of Śabda and Artha, i.e. not different from the Śabda and the Artha, denoted by it. At this stage Vaiyākaraṇas believe that the so called Śakti (capacity) is nothing but the relation of expressive and expressed (or Vācya-Vācaka) between a Śabda and Artha. The entire transaction in the world is based on this relation. Śabda is the substratum of the transaction.

Notes : Pratibhbā is a unique type of intelligence. Its another form is the Vākyārtha (verbal meaning). The worldly transaction is in the form of intelligence. It is not concerned with outer world. In outer world, the same thing is treated/undrstood/perceived differently by people. The same lady is considered by-a lustful man as a thing of enjoyment, tiger etc. as somthing edible, parents as daughter, her children as mother and those who renounced the world as a dead-body. The cause for such different considerations is the 'Samskāra' (refinement) in their mind. Śabda is the very cause of all this.

Moreover those things which do not exist in outer world are also there in verbal-transaction (for instance skyflower). They are denoted by Śabda.

Similarly, those things without concrete shape in the world are also denoted by Śabda (example-ātmā). The difference between a cloth and pot is also originated from Śabda.

Therefore, the entire universe is subject to Pratibhā. The Śabda applies to a thing which does not exist in the world. Śabda transforms into the universe. This concept is explained in verse 13 in this Kāṇḍa.

Intro : The idea given in the last verse *is being detailed* –

षड्जादिभेदः शब्देन व्याख्यातो रूप्यते यतः।
तस्मादर्थविधास्सर्वाः शब्दमात्रासु निश्रिताः।।

119. ṣadjādibhedāḥ śabdena vyākhyāto rūpyate yataḥ
tasmādarthavidhassarvaḥ śabdamātreṣu niśritam

Sum : Since, it is seen that distinctions between two things, for instance, between ṣadja and another musical note, becomes clear when explained only through Śabda. Therefore, manner of things is determined only through Śabdas.
Com : In Gāndharvaśāstra seven kinds of Dhvanis are defined (Niṣāda, ṚṢabha, Gāndhāra, Ṣaḍja, Madhyama, Dhaivata, and Pañcama). The definitions of these Dhvanis or Svaras are in the form of Śabda. Without Śabda, it is not possible to distinguish between any two of the above Dhvanis.

Pot, cloth etc. are clearly perceived by us. But the difference among such things is based on Śabda only.
Notes : Cowherds, shepherds etc., who take care of animals call them in peculiar fashions. A specific herd is called in a specific manner and the animals respond. Therefore, the entire transaction in the universe is dependent on Śabda.
Intro : The author says that *the very creation of Universe is caused by Śabda*

शब्दस्य परिणामोऽयमित्याम्नायविदो विदुः ।
छन्दोभ्य एव प्रथममेतद्विश्वं व्यवर्तत ।।

120. śabdasya pariṇāmoyamityāmnāyavido viduḥ
chandobhya eva prathamametadviśvam vyavartata

Sum : Those who are versed in Vedas know that this Universe is the transformation of Speech. It was out of Vedas that this Universe was evolved.
Com : The Universe is the evolution of Śabda-say those who know the purport of Vedas. It is clrealy stated in Vedas, Smṛtis and Purāṇas, which are based on Vedas, that the Universe is evolved out of Vedas.
Notes : The Vaiyākaraṇas believe in the Upaniṣadic theory that the unity with the unqualified-secondless-Brahman (Nirguṇādvayabrahma-bhāva) is Mokṣa. or salvation. So they too follow the evolution theory (Vivartavāda). Therefore, here in this verse the word Pariṇāma means evolution.
Intro : It is said that the Universe, which consists of ghaṭa etc., is the evolution of Śabda. In such a case how is it that the form of clay is seen in a pot, made of clay, but not that of Śabda ? – the author responds that it is acceptable to us, it's *the conclusion of Grammarians* (Vaiyākaraṇasiddhānta), and it is experienced –

इतिकर्तव्यता लोके सर्वा शब्दव्यपाश्रया ।
यं पूर्वाहितसंस्कारो बालोऽपि प्रतिपद्यते ।।

121. itikartavyatā loke sarvā śabdavyapāsrayā
yam pūrvāhitasamskāro bālo'pi pratipadyate

Sum : In the Universe, the 'itikartavyatā' (the imagination that a work has to be done like this), which even a boy, due to his refinement (Samskāra) in his last birth, is able to grasp, is based on Śabda.

Com : Kartavya means the work to be done. The imagination that this work has to be done like this-is 'itikartavyatā'. Such imagination is absolutely based on Śabda. Therefore, the itikartavyatā is there, related to each object (padārtha). Without such an imagination, it is not possible for anybody to do anything. Such an imagination is a mental process and the same may not be audible to others. But in the mind of the thinker it reveals itself in the form of Śabda. Like the (dry) clay, the Śabda is also there inevitably in a pot.

Soon after the birth the boy is without the knowledge of Śabda. Nevertheless, he can do the Verbal-imaginations (Śabdabhāvanā) at the young age due to the refinement (Samskāra) attained from last birth.

Notes : The physical structure may change but the spirit (Jīvaśakti),, an inherent quality, follows the chain of births uninterrupted. In order to experience the nemesis, one gets another birth. The concept is elaborated in verse 122.

Intro : How to ascertain that a child has got the so called 'itikartavyatā ? – the author answers the question –

आद्यः करणविन्यासः प्राणस्योर्ध्वं समीरणम् ।
स्थानानामभिघातश्च न विना शब्दभावनाम ।।

122. ādyaḥ karaṇavinyāsaḥ prāṇasyordhvam samīraṇam
sthānānāmabhighātaśca na vinā śabdabhāvanām

Sum : That first movement of the organs (of speech), the upward sending of breath and its contact with the centers-these would not be possible but for verbal imagination (in the child).

Notes : 'Śabdas are to be pronounced like this and these are Śabdas-without such a knowledge a child makes an effort through different parts of the body-he chokes the breath, tightens the vocal chords, swallows the saliva and stretches the jaws, and so on. Without these efforts the pronunciation of Śabdas is not possible.

Moreover, by nature air travells horizontally and in spite of that the child tries to push the Prāṇavāyu upwards and also passes the same through the speech-centres.

Since, the child makes all the above efforts, it can be confirmed that it imagines the Śabda. But, as it is not trained in these efforts in this birth but has got the equipment, the cause behind is nothing but the refinement of its last birth (Pụrvajanmasamskāra). Therefore, generally Śabda is the criterion of itikartavyatā.

Intro : The author states that not only in the verbal knowledge but also *in the knowledge in general too the Śabda permeates –*

न सोऽस्ति प्रत्ययो लोके यश्शब्दानुगमादृते।
अनुविद्धमिव ज्ञानं सर्वं शब्देन भासते।।

123. na so'sti pratyayo loke yaśśabdānugamād ṛte
anuviddhamiva jñānam sarvam śabdena bhāsate

Sum : In this world no knowledge is possible except as accompanied by Śabda. All types of knowledge (due to percection, inference etc). shines as permeated by speech.

Com : Any knowledge is accompanie by Śabda. Without the relation of Śabda no knowledge exists. Firstly, the speaker discerns the meaning in the mind and also the appropriate Śabda. In accordance with the idea he imagines the relation between Śabda and Artha. All this process is based on Śabda. When he wishes to express the idea to others he takes the Śabda as a gate. The listner also grasps the meaning through Śabda only. This concept is detailed in verse 53.

That's why, all types of knowledge, i.e. perceptive inferential, assimilative, verbal, recollective and illusive, shines, mixed with Śabda. In day to day transaction it is difficult to find knowledge free of verbal relation. Here in this verse 'pratyaya' means cognition/knowledge.

Intro : The author substantiates the fact that *knowledge is accompanied by Śabda* in some form or the other –

वाग्रूपता चेन्निष्क्रामेत् अवबाधस्य शाश्वती।
न प्रकाशः प्रकाश्येत सा हि प्रत्यवमर्शिनी।।

124. vāgrūpatā cenniṣkrāmedavabodhasya sasvatī
na prakāśah prakāśyeta sā hi pratyavamarśini

Sum : If the natural relation between speech and knowledge goes away then the knowledge would not shine, as it is the Śabda which is to be employed to transform knowledge to others.

Com : One cannot know the idea another has got in mind. That has to be revealed only through Śabda. If Śabda, a luminating agent, were not there, one could have not been in a position to transform his knowledge to others. It may not be amiss to conclude that one's own knowledge should have not been shined as, if one has some knowledge he has to imagine the same only through Śabda.

When one attains some knowledge, he imagines 'I got the knowledge'. As soon as one perceives a pot he gets the knowledge of pot. 'I know the pot' – the knowledge in this form is anuvyavasāya. The minute form is also similar to this.

The transformation of once attained knowledge is called 'pratyavamarśa'. It's in the form of Śabda.

Intro : Bhartṛhari asserts that *everything in the Universe is the evolution of Śabda*

सा सर्वविद्या शिल्पानां कलानां चोपबन्धनी।
तद्वशादभिनिष्पन्नं सर्वं वस्तु विभज्यते।।

125. sā sarvavidyāśilpānām kalānāmcopabandhanī
tadvaśādabhinispannam sarvam vastu vibhajyate

Sum : It is speech which binds all branches of knowledge of Arts and Crafts. Evertyhting is produced and classified through its capacity.

Com : People participate in mundane functions as well as Vedic rites in case they like, and keep themselves aloof in case of dislike. The participation and non-participation (pravṛtti and nivṛtti) are based on the (fourteen) branches of knowledge – Arts and Crafts. Animals, birds and non-living things like pot, cloth etc. are under the command of the man. The cause behind this is the gamut of all branches of knowledge, Arts and Crafts.

The branches of knowledge Arts and Crafts are there in the mind of the teacher in minute form. If these things are to be transformed into the mind of the desciple Śabda is the very useful instrument. Such a Śabda is in the form of knowledge. Otherwise, it would have been possible by simple pronunciation of Śabda. The desciple is able to grasp the knowledge. Therefore Śabda and Jnana (knowledge) are identical. Since Śabda and Artha are identical, as soon as the teacher pronounces the Śabda, the student gets the knowledge of Artha.

Notes : Moreover, each thing initially takes shape in the form of minute Śabda in the mind of a man and the same thing appears in concrete form in outside world. That' swhy the things are distinguished from each other through words like ghaṭa (pot) paṭa (cloth) etc. Due to the said reason only it has become possible that the same individual is treated/looked differently by different people. This concept it elaborated back in verse 118.

Therefore, various branches of knowledge – Arts and Crafts, and the differentiation of each thing in the Universe is based on the form of Śabda.

Intro : Śabda is not only the base of different branches of knowledge-Arts and Crafts, but also *it is another form of Śabda, which is called, caitanya* (or consciousness) that exists in all the beings says the author –

सैषा संसारिणां संज्ञा बहिरन्तश्च वर्तते।
तन्मात्रमनतिक्रान्तं चैतन्यं सर्वजन्तुषु।।

126. saiṣā samsāriṇām samjñā bahirantaśca vartate
tanmātramanatikrāntam caitanyam sarvajantuṣu

Sum : This speech exists within and outside all living beings in the form of consciousness. It's so because the consciousness in all the living beings is certainly preceded by speech.

Com : Each being thinks/feels-I'm happy, I'm worried, I'm working etc. The consciousness is the cause behind all such thinking. People speak and interact with eachother. Caitanya is the cause behind it. Such a Caitanya is in the form of Śabda as people carry on transactions through Śabda only.

Notes : There are Jātis like ghaṭatva and paṭatva in Vyaktis (individuals) like ghaṭa and paṭa. They are all dependent on the form of Śabda. There is no Jāti without Śabda.

Even trees etc. do experience the happiness and sorrow. Rather they know their own feelings but cannot express other's feelings. They are living things as they grow again after cut down.

Intro : Śabda is the consciousness of human beings – the author substantiates the idea –.

अर्थक्रियासु वाक् सर्वान् समीहयति देहिनः ।
तदुत्क्रान्तौ विसंज्ञोऽयं दृश्यते काष्ठकुड्यवत् ।।

127. arthakriyāsu vāk sarvān samīhayati dehiḥ
tadutkrāntau visamjño'yam dṛśyate kāṣṭhakuḍyavat

Sum : It is speech (in the form of consciousness) which prompts all mankind to activity. When it is gone, man, being unconscious looks like a log of wood or a piece of stone.

Com : The Śabda prompts the human beings in different deeds. According to the need, everyone, firstly understands, then have a desire, endeavours to get it and finally moves to and fro. This order (called jānāti, icchati, yatate,cesṭate) is followed by people in all transactions. Jānāti, is the first among them. That is Śabda. The same is consciousness or caitanya. Those things, like tree, and creeper, which do not have such a relation with Śabda are not able to move as the human beings do.

As soon as the sabda passes away from the body, it remains like other unconscious things, i.e. a log of wood, a piece of stone, a wall etc. Such a situation is seen in a state like deep sleep (suṣupti), fainting and death.

Intro : Having eestablished the Śabda is the cause of all transactions during waking state, now the author emphasises that *during dreaming state also the same is the cause*

प्रविभागे यथा कर्ता तथा कार्ये प्रवर्तते ।
अविभागे तथा सैव कार्यत्वेनावतिष्ठते ।।

128. Pravibhāge yathā kartā tathā kārye pravartate
avibhāge tathā saiva kāryatvenāvatiṣṭhate

Sum : It is speech through which an agent functions in connection with an object in the state of wakefulness. But during the state of dream, it is again the speech which manifests itself in the form of subject, object and instrument (since the agent would not be able to distinguish among the said three factors).

Com : Śabda or caitanya is the sole factor that causes functioning of every being during waking state in any transaction. The human beings function through speech with caitanya in the form of Śabda. This idea is stated clearly in verse 127.

Similarly Śabda is useful during the state of dream where one would not be able to distinguish among subject, object and instrument. The remarkable thing is that during the dreaming state the caitanya in the form of Śabda itelf manifests as the functioning subject, functioned object and as a useful instrument in the function. During the state of dream all things are in the form of sub-conscious impression and not in concrete form as they are during the state of waking. Therefore they are called prātibhāsikas (illusory). One may dream a journey on a chariot. In truth there is neither a chariot nor horses. All that happens through Śabda. During the state of waking Śabda is the instrument. During the State of dream it functions as an instrument as well as an object.

During the state of dream the conciousness or caitanya functions on behalf of all the sense-organs. It was stated in verse 125 that Śabda itself is caitanya.

Intro : The author states that the *evolution in the universe is absolutely related to Śabda –*

स्वमात्रा परमात्रा वा श्रुत्या प्रक्रम्यते यथा।
तथैव रूढतामेति तथा ह्यर्थो विधीयते।।

129. svamātr ā paramātrā vā srutyā prakramyate yathā
tathaiva rūḍhatāmeti tayā hyartho vidhīyate

Sum : Whether one object is shown as two or two objects shown as one, it is the Śabda which establishes objects in the form of knowledge. The Śabda establishes the meaning (in the form of knowledge) of things in the mind.

Com : There is the sentence-'Rāhoḥ śiraḥ' (the head of Rāhu). An individual was cut into two, head and trunk (with hands and legs) and the head is named Rāhu whereas the rest is called Ketu. Therefore the head itelf is Rāhu, and there are no other parts (of the body). Nevertheless, the above sentence is there very much in usage.

The Śabda insinuates that there are two parts of the same head. This is the greatness of Śabda.

Similarly, in Vyākaraṇa the Sthānyādeśa (original-substitute) process is there. In truth, the Sthānī is differnt and the Ādeśa is different too. The Śāstra says that Ādeśa is akin to Sthānī. In this case two different things are considered identical due to Śabda.

The Śabda makes Artha in different forms, the subject of mind, without any contact with the things in the outer world.

Intro : The concept of the last verse *is being elaborated –*

अत्यन्तमतथाभूते निमित्ते श्रुत्युपाश्रयात्।
दृश्यतेऽलातचक्रादौ वस्त्वाकारनिरूपणा।।

130. atyantamatathābhūte nimitte śrutyupāśrayāt
drśyate'lātacakrādau vastvākāranirūpaṇā

Sum : Even when the cause for verbal expression (i.e. an object) is entirely non-existent, discription of the form of such a thing through Śabdas is found, as in the case of a circle made by a firebrand.

Com : The Śabda, being grasped by the ear, makes the Artha, in itself, subject to mind. It may not be surprising if Śabda, which becomes subject to mind through ear, makes the meaning in itself, subject to mind. Śabda is suggestive (pratyāyaka) and the meaning is there in it in the form of suggestive (pratyāyya). While noting the thing, the Śabda becomes instrumental without consideration to the very existence of that particular thing (Artha), in the outer world. The criterion for such a state is the desire of the speaker (to say) or commonly known as Vivakṣā.

A lot of process is involved here – the wheel of a chariot is visible as well as tangible. It is tangible on all sides simultaneously. On the other hand the whirling of a fire-brand is quite different. The fire-brand, when whirled looks like a whirling. Rather, we are certain that such a whirling does not exist at all, since, although it is visible, it is not tangible at all sides simultaneously. Therefore, it can be concluded that since it is tangible a wheel of a chariot is an existing-thing and a whirling of a fire-brand is a non-existing thing. Nevertheless, the Śabda, i.e. Alātacakra, (the whirling of a fire-brand) denotes the latter.

Notes : Similarly, Vandhyāputra (the son of a barren-woman), Śaśaśṛnga (the horn of a harem), Gaganakusuma (a sky-flower) etc. are also meaningful Śabdas, rather such things are not there in the Universe.

Intro : Vedas hold that the Paramātmā is the cause of the entire Universe. In case it is argued that Śabda is the cause of the Universe, the Vedic concept cannot be held up-in response to this the author says that the *Śabda is a form of Paramātmā* –

अपि प्रयोक्तुरात्मानं शब्दमन्तरवस्थितम्।
प्राहुर्महान्तमृषभं येन सायुज्यमिष्यते।।

131. api prayokturātmānam śabdamantaravasthitam
prāhurmahāntamṛṣabham yena sāyujyamiṣyate

Sum : Moreover, speech, which exists whithin the speaker as his self is said to be the great Bull, identity with which is desired (by those who have renounced the world).

Com : Vedic hymns praise the greatness of Śabda, which is in the form of big Bull (Vṛṣabda). The Śabda can satisfy any desire. It is all-powerful and a form of Paramātmā (Universal-soul). The human beings are filled with such a Śabda. The saints (those who desire Mokṣa or salvation) can get identity with the same if they serve. Its real form can be known through the study of Vyākaraṇa. Such a study would destroy the sins, and thru Dharma purifies the mind, which will effect the identity of the student (of Vyākaraṇa) with the unqualified-nondual-Brahman (the universal soul).

Intro : The author *offers a device* to unite with the Śabdabrahman –

तस्मात् यश्शब्दसंस्कारः सा सिद्धिः परमात्मनः
तस्य प्रवृत्तितत्वज्ञः तद्ब्रह्मामृतमश्नुते ।।

132. tasmāt yaśśabdasamskāraḥ sā siddhiḥ paramātmanha
tasya pravṛttitattvajñaḥ tadbrahmāmṛtamaśnute

Sum : Therefore, attainment of impeccable speech is the attainemnt of Brahman. He who knows the secret of its functioning enjoys the immortal Brahman.

Com : The effect of correct Śabdas (Sādhu-Śabdas) is reduced due to their contact with incorrect Śabdas (Asādhu-Śabdas). Therefore, they cnnot render Dharma. So firstly one must distinguish Sādhuśabdas from Asādhuśabdas. The same is called Śabdasamskāra. Through this the sins are desctoyed. Dharma is increased, and the mind is purified. Then only the one could attain salvation (mokṣa), described in Upaniṣads, in the form of identity with unqualified Brahman.

Notes : The Śabdabrahman undergoes all the six alterations. viz. Jāyate (produces), Asti (exists), Vipariṇamate (changes), Vardhate (grows), Apakṣīyate (erodes), Vinaśyati (Perishes)-(Ref. Nirukta, 1-28, 29). The same are called Pravṛttis. The noumenon of the same is the invariable Brahman itself.

The Sādhuśabda is also an alteration. One would attain Pratibhā (intuition) in case he is careful about correct Śabda. Such a knowledge of Sādhuśabdas is bound with Vyākaraṇa. Without Vyākaraṇa the real form of Śabda cannot be known. This idea is discussed in verse 13. Right from verse 118 to this verse the greatness of Śabda is elaborated.

Intro : Through the usage of Sādhuśabda one would attain Dharma, through that the purity of mind and eventually the Mokṣa (salvation) – it is stated. But how can the Vyākaraṇasmṛti can be an authority ? It cannot be authoritative since it is personal (Pauruṣeya)-in order to clear the doubt the author says that not only Vyākaraṇa but also *all the scriptures* (Smṛtis) *are based on Vedas* –

न जात्वकर्तृकं कश्चिदागमं प्रतिपद्यते।
बीजं सर्वागमापाये त्रय्येवातो व्यवस्थिता ।।

133. na jātvakartṛkaṁ kaścidāgamam pratipadyate
bījam sarvāgamāpāye trayyevāto vyavasthitā

Sub : No one considers the Smṛtis (Scriptures) to be of impersonal origin. When all such Scriptures perish, the three Vedas alone exist as the base (of all Scriptures).

Com : Everyone does not consider the Smṛtis to be impersonal (Apauruṣeya) like Vedas. One would rather think that they are man-made. It means that since they are mortal they would certainly perish. Sādhuśabdaprayoga would help in the attainment of salvation. Vyākaraṇa, athough man-made, is authoritative since it is based on Vedas and for that matter any Smṛti is authoritive as each one is based on Vedas. The author substantiates this view in ten verses i.e. from 133-143.

Note : The Smṛtis that are found today are built by sages (Ṛṣis) depending on the Vedic knowledge and not independently using their intuition. Hindus believe that Vedas are the absolute authority.

Everybody believes that Smṛtis are man-made. Nobody trusts that they are impersonal or superhuman, i.e. since they are man-made they are non-eternal. During pralaya (deluge) they will perish.

After the Deluge at the begining of Yuga, Kapila etc. sages compose Smṛtis based on Vedas. Veda survives the Deluge. It is immortal. The above one is a recurring process. Vyākaraṇa is one of the Smṛtis and therefore is athoritative. So the above concept is genuine.

Intro : When the personal (man-made) Smṛtis perish and since their base viz. Vedas, are unknown, *the practice of Dharma is interrupted during that period* – the author clarifies the doubt –

अस्तंयातेपु वादेपु कर्तृष्वन्यप्वसत्स्वपि।
श्रुतिस्मृत्युदितं धर्मं लोको न व्यतिवर्तते ।।

134. astam yāteṣu vādeṣu kartṛṣvanyeṣvasatsvapi
śrutismṛtyuditam dharmam loko na vyativartate

Sum : Even when different schools (of Āgamas) perish and there are no new authors, mankind does not transgress the duties prescribed by the Vedas and the Smṛtis.

Com : During Deluge all the Smṛtis perish. The authors do die. At the begining of Yuga there were no authors. Therefore, one may be in doubt that during the interval the practice of Dharma might have been disrupted. But, in fact, the Śiṣṭas (those who observe vedic rituals etc.) do go on practising Dharma. Therefore there won't be any disruption to the performance of Dharma.

Intro : Bhartṛhari answers the following question – The knowledge of Dharma and Adharma attributed to (Kapila etc.) sages is intuitive. Neither other Smṛtis nor Vedas have anything to do with it. Then *how can it be possible to argue that Smṛtis have their roots in Vedas ?* –

ज्ञाने स्वाभाविके नार्थः शास्त्रैः कश्चन विद्यते।
धर्मो ज्ञानस्य हेतुश्चेत्तस्याम्नायो निबन्धनम्।।

135. Jñāne svābhāvike nārthaḥ śāstraiḥ kaścana vidyate
dharmo jñānasya hetuścettasyāmnāyo nibandhanam

Sum : If knowledge were intuitive, then scriptures are of no use, but if virtue is the root of knowledge then the source of knowledge is the Veda.

Com : Even people other than Kapila etc. sages may posses intuitive knowledge related to Dharma and Adharma (without consulting Vedas). So, the works of the sages meant for others are useless. Therefore, it is logical to conclude that the knowledge preserved in smṛtis has got its roots in Vedas. So much so that it is a fact that smṛtis have their origin in Vedas and the knowledge of Kapila etc. sages is not intuitive.

It is not trustworthy that Dharma graces only those like Kapila etc. and not others. So sages like Kapila have studied Vedas in detail, observed the Vedic rituals and thus gained more and more knowledge. They put the facts and findings in a nutshell for the sake of common people, who cannot understand the intensive meaning of Vedas.

Intro : It is proved that smṛtis are authoritative since they are composed on the basis of Vedic principles. In such a case, when there are Vedas to render necessary knowledge, is not the *composition of Pūrvamīmāmsā and Uttaramīmāmsā, separately,* a vain attempt ? Bhartṛhari clarifies –

वेदशास्त्राविरोधी च तर्कश्चक्षुरपश्यताम्।
रूपमात्राद्धि वाक्यार्थः केवलान्नावतिष्ठते।।

136. vedaśāstrāvirodhī ca tarkaścakṣurapaśyatām
rūpamātrāddhi vākyārthaḥ kevalānnāvatiṣṭhate

Sum : The Pūrva-Uttara-Mīmāmsas, which are not contradictory to the Vedas, called Śāstra, are an eye to those who do not possess the vision (into the significance of Vedas). The sense of a (Vedic) sentence is not obtained from its own form itself.

Com : This verse explains the very purpose of Śāstras. Here the word 'tarka' refers to Pūrvamīmāmsā founded by Jaimini and Uttaramīmāmsā founded by Vedavyāsa.

In Vedic texts the meaning of certain sentences is inconsistent and doubtful. We, common people cannot conceive the exact meaning and draw conclusions. Such Vedic texts are analysed with pros and cons and the purport is decided by Pūrvamīmāmsā and Uttaramīmāmsā. The meaning of Vedic sentences is vague and Śāstras make it clear. Without the help of Śāstras we cannot fathom the meaning.

Śāstra is helpful in understanding Vedārtha, like the eye in perceiving objects. Such a Śāstra should not be contrary to Vedas. The 'viruddha-tarka' (anti-ta ka) cannot decide the very meaning. Therefore, the Vedārtha has to be decided, through Tarka.

Intro : The author illustrates the concept that *Tarka is essential to decide the purport of Vedic texts –*

सतोऽविवक्षा पारार्थ्यं व्यक्तिरर्थस्य लैङ्गिकी ।
इति न्यायो बहुविधस्तर्केण प्रविभज्यते ।।

137. satóvivakṣāpārārthyam vyaktirarthasya laiṅgikī
iti nyāyo bahuvidhastarkeṇa pravibhajyate

Sum : Various kinds of means of interpretting sentences have been classified by Tarka, such as, for instance-the intended meaning of a sentence (is such and such) in a statement is for a purpose different (from what is obvious) and a meaning becomes clear from the evidence of another sentence.

Com : At times, we have to construe the Vedic texts without taking into account the primary meaning of the same and in some instances the otherway round. It is not possible for us to decide as to where and whcih way we have to follow. The task is fullfilled by Tarka.

Notes : The following maxim of Pāṇini can be an example –

Tasyāpatyam (4-1-92) = the Taddhita suffix 'aṇ' becomes applicable to the stem in possessive case, if offspring is the meaning. The term 'tasya' denotes that the suffix applies to the stem which is in masculine gender and in singular number. So (Daśarathasya apatyam =) Dāśarathiḥ etc. forms only can be attained. The suffix will not be applicable to the stems in feminine gender and with dual and plural numbers. So (Sumitrāyāḥ apatyam) = Saumitriḥ, (svasroḥ apatye =) svasrīyau etc. forms cannot be effected. Similarly, since the Śabda 'apatyam' denotes only singlular number, the maxim does not apply, in case the offspring is more than one (in dual and plural number). So much so that it has to be concluded that the gender and number in the above Sūtra are unaccountable (not important).

The famous sentence 'Kākebhyo dadhi rakṣyatām' (protect the curd from crows) is another example. Where the purport is important rather than the primarily indicated meaning. The term 'Kākebhyaḥ' suggests the connotation. Therefore, anyone, i.e. cat, dog, etc., that spoils the curd has to be taken as the meaning of the Śabda, 'kāka', rather than (only) crow itself. On the other hand, it means that the curd need not be protected from other curd-spoiling agents. So much so that the Śabda kāka' in the above sentence denotes all the agents that spoil the curd. The same purport is precisely put as 'Dadhyupaghātake Kākapadam lākṣaṇikam' (The Śabda 'Kāka' is indicative of all the curd-spoiling agents). Here the Śabda 'Kāka' is technically called 'Upalakṣaṇam' (indicator). The sentence 'Abhirūpāya Kanyā deyā (a virgin has to be offered to one who is compatible) expresses the general meaning. After the study of some more precepts it is decided that a virgin has to be offered to one with education, wealth, good-appearance, caste etc. and the same meaning is considered to be that of the quoted sentence.

In the same manner there are so many instances where conclusions are drawn through Tarka.

Intro : The power of Śabda is the root of the Tarka explained by human-beings. On the other hand, that Tarka offered independently by human-beings is called Śuṣka-tarka (dry-logic). *Such a Tarka, says the author, cannot decide the purport of Vedas –*

शब्दानामेव सा शक्तिः तर्को यः पुरुषाश्रयः ।
शब्दाननुगतो न्यायोऽनागमेष्वनिबन्धनः ।।

138. śabdānāmeva sā śaktiḥ tarko yaḥ puruṣāśrayaḥ
śabdānanugato nyāyo 'nāgameṣvanibandhanaḥ

Sum : Human reasoning is the power of Śabda. That reasoning is in acceptance with the scriptures. The reasoning which is given by the persons who do not respect the power of Śabda or which is against the power of Śabda cannot be authentic in deciding the purport of a Śabda (sentence, text etc.).

Com : 'Tasyāpatyam', 'Kākebhyo dadhi rakṣyatam', 'Abhirūpāya Kanyā deyā', etc. sentences are pregnant with meaning given in the earlier verse. Persons are not attributing any meaning that is not related to the sentence. Rather, They give reasoning in order to make the hidden meaning clear.

On the other hand, if anyone interprets a Śabda, keeping away the power of Śabda, then such an interpretation is not considered to be authentic by Prāmāṇikas (authoritative people). The interpretation is rediculed as dry-logic (Śuṣka-tarka).

Intro : Before going to state that the Sādhuśabdas can produce Dharma (in verse 140), the author gives *two examples in support of his statement* : –

रूपादयो यथा दृष्टाः प्रत्यर्थं यतशक्तयः ।
शब्दास्तथैव दृश्यन्ते विषापहरणादिषु ।।

139. rūpādayo yathā dṛṣṭaḥ pratyartham yataśaktayaḥ
śabdāstathaiva dṛśyante viṣāpaharaṇādiṣu

Sum : Just as different colors etc. are found to possess certain capacities towards different things (objects), so are the Śabdas or Hymns in Vedas found (to possess the capacity) in destroying poison etc.

Com : We look the form with the eyes. It is also useful in distinguishing among colours and shades like blue, green etc.. But 'Bhāsvaraśukla' (brilliant white) destroys the eyes and as such it cannot be seen with eyes. Therefore, although the form can generally be seen, there is difference in the effect.

Sweetness causes the phlem to increase. The essence of pepper, chilly powder (hot in taste) increases Paitya (biliousness ?) The smell of venomous herbs causes fainting. The smell of Mālatī makes one overactive.

It is stated in Āyurveda that (intercourse with) young girl increases the longevity, a lady in youth helps in saving the longevity, a lady in prime youth and well-versed in the art of sexual enjoyment (called Prauḍha) causes one to become old early (the longevity is reduced) and an old woman leads to (early) death. (bālā prāṇapradā proktā yuvatī prāṇadhāriṇī

prauḍhā karoti vṛddhatvam vṛddhā maraṇamādiśet)

Similarly, in Atharvaveda there are certain Mantras which would work as antidotes to venoms of scorpion, snake etc., Some would ruin the enemy. Śrīsūkta and Puruṣasūkta in Ṛgveda help in attaining God's grace.

Rūpādi means rūpa (form), rasa (essence or taste), gandha (smell) and sparśa (touch).

Intro : The author *applies the given example* in the present context-

यथैषां तत्र सामर्थ्यं धर्मोऽप्येवं प्रतीयताम् ।
साधूनां साधुभिस्तस्माद्वाच्यमभ्युदयार्थिनाम् ।।

140. yathaiṣām tatra sāmarthyam dharmo' pyevam pratīyatām
sāḍhūnām sādhubhistasmādvācyamabhyudayārthinām

Sum : Just as these Śabdas have power to do that, so are they understood (as possessing capacity) in regard to virtuous conduct. Therefore, correct Śabdas must be employed by those desirous of elevative (both in this world as well as in heaven after death).

Com : Rūpa, rasa, gandha, sparśa and the Mantras in Atharvaṇa are effective in different ways, So also the Sādhuśabdas in attaining Dharma. Their purpose may be expression of meaning and it is the dṛṣṭaphala (visible result). Dharma is another purpose which is an adṛṣṭaphala (invisible result).

Therefore, one who is desirous of Dharma should employ only correct Śabdas in common parlance also.

Intro : Some Śabdas have the capacity to work as antidotes against poison and it is a matter of perception, whereas, the argument that Sādhuśabdas produce Dharma-cannot be proved on the basis of perception. Then *how can the above theory be sustainable* ? the author answers the question –

सर्वोऽदृष्टफलानर्थानागमात् प्रतिपद्यते ।
विपरीतं च सर्वत्र शक्यते वक्तुमागमे ।।

141. sarvo 'dṛṣṭaphalānarthānāgamāt pratipadyate
viparītam ca sarvatra śakyate vaktumāgame

Sum : Men learn about matters, which have transcendental effects, from Vedas. The argument that contrary results can also be expected is applicable to the entire Veda (which is not desirable).

Com : People learn subjects (which can be perceived through sense-organs) through sense-organs only and the transcendental subjects like Yāgas (Sacrifices), which lead to Svarga (heaven) through Vedas. Veda says 'one desirous of Svarga has to perform Sacrifice (Svargakāmo yajeta). There is no otherway to know such things.

A doubt : Why not Sādhuśabdas cause Adharma ? It is also an adṛṣṭaphala (invisible result). How to decide that Sādhuśabdas produce Dharma only ? – the author answers these questions in the latter half of the verse-Donations produce Puṇya (merit), thefting causes sin-such things are stated in Vedas. One can argue that contrary results can also happen through the actions and it can be applied to the entire gamut of actions specified in Vedas. In such a case nothing can be trustworthy. Therefore, such a reasoning is not desirable. People can carry on their daily business properly only when they believe in Vedas, regarding merit and sin (Puṇya and Pāpa).

Intro : Vyākaraṇaśāstra is a Smṛti (code of law). This Smṛti only can serve the purpose of distinguishing Sādhuśabdas from Asādhu-śabdas. It is established through Siṣṭaparamparā (the chain of śiṣṭas). Therefore, the author says, *Vyākaraṇa can be authoritative in stating that Dharma can be achieved through the usage of Sādhuśabdas* (correct Śabdas) –

साधुत्वज्ञानविषया सैषा व्याकरणस्मृतिः ।
अविच्छेदेन शिष्टानामिदं स्मृतिनिबन्धनम् ।।

142. sādhutvajñānaviṣayā saiṣā vyākaraṇasmṛtiḥ
avicchedena śiṣṭānāmidam smṛtinibandhanam

Sum : This tradition of Grammar has the knowledge of correctness as its subject. And it is directly based on the unbroken (series of) recollections of learned men.

Com : The Sādhuśabdas, that have been pronounced by Śiṣṭas, since time immemorial, are inherited through successive learned men down through the ages and are thus perpetuated. The Vyākaraṇa is based on such Sādhuśabdas (Prayogaśaraṇam Vyākaraṇam = Vyākaraṇa is based on usage of Śabdas) and not new-ones.

The sages, who know the noumenon of Śabda, have discerned, decided and devided the Śadhu and Asādhuśabdas. Following these decisions only Pāṇini, Kātyāyana and Patañjali have brought this Vyākaraṇa for the people. This alone would decide the correctness of Śabda. Therefore, we need not search for anythingelse in this regard.

Notes : This Vyākaraṇa gives Sādhuśabdas that have come down as a legacy through successive gurus (teachers), in so many ways. Hence, some Śabdas, although they seem to be correct in terms of Pāṇini-sūtras, are seperated and stamped to be unfit for usage. For example Patañjali says 'Na hi vaciran-tiparaḥ prayujyate' (The root Vac is not used with the suffix 'anti'). There are many similar instances.

Intro : Having projected the Vyākaraṇa as an authority, the author explains *the subject of Vyākaraṇa, i.e., the Śabdasvarūpa* (the form of Śabda) –

वैखर्या मध्यमायाश्च पश्यन्त्याश्चैतदद्भुतम् ।
अनेकतीर्थभेदायाः त्रय्या वाचः परं पदम् ।।

143. vaikharyā madhyamāyāśca paśyantyāścaitadadbhutam
anekatīrthabhedāyāstrayyā vācaḥ param padam

Sum : It is the best and unique source of speech, which is situated at three places and which is of three-fold, viz. Vaikhary, Madhyamā and Paśyantī.

Com : Śabda is there in three places, viz. throat, consciousness (Prāṇa) and mind (Buddhi). It has got three parts, viz. Vaikhary, Madhyamā and Paśyantī. Vyākaraṇa is an instrument to know all these forms of Sabda.

Notes : In verse 44, the author said that two types of Śabdas, i.e., Vaikhary and Madhyamā are the subject of Vyākaraṇa. It is said so keeping inview the common people like us. For us, Śabda, only in these two forms would be the subject of experience. We cannot identify Paśyantī. It can be experienced by Yogins only. Keeping in view the Yogins, Bhartṛhari said 'trayyāḥ' (of the three types). Parāvāk is such that even Yogins cannot identify. It is beyond anybody's purview, that is the unqualified Brahman, itself. Therefore, Bhartṛhari left it and said 'trayyāḥ'. So, one should not conclude that speech is only of three types. It is clearly stated in works like Ṛgvedabhāṣya, Mahābhārata, Śivadṛṣṭi, Kāmakalāvilāsa etc., that the Vāk is of four types. The root and suffix analysis is there in Paśyantī also. It is available to Yogins.

Vaikhary is that which is pronounced by the movement of throat (vocal chords), lips etc.. This is audible to others. Madhyamā is that which is there in the mind. Madhyamā is eternal. Vaikhary is produced. Vaikhary manifests Madhyamā . Madhyamāśabda is suitable for application of Grammatical functions. Madhyamā as well as Paśyantī are directly the subject of Vyākaraṇa. Since it is suggestive of Madhyamā, Vaikhary also becomes the subject of Vyākaraṇa.

Intro : As it was explained in the earlier verse, *Vyākaraṇa is a device to know the Sādhuśabdas*. The author emphasises the concept –

तद्विभागाविभागाभ्यां क्रियमाणमवस्थितम् ।
स्वभावज्ञैश्च भावानां दृश्यन्ते शब्दशक्तयः ।।

144. tadvibhāgāvibhāgābhyām kriyamāṇamavasthitam
svabhāvajñaiśca bhāvānām dṛśyante śabdaśaktayaḥ

Sum : That Vyākaraṇa is seen as being constructed by two different features, viz. the treatment (of Śabdas) in analitical terms or as integral parts. The capacities of Śabdas are noticed by sages, who were well-versed in the attributes of Padārthas.

Com : The sages with transcendental knowledge have discerned the virtues of -expression of meaning as well as producing Dharma-in Śabdas and through Vyākaraṇa they handed down such Śabdas to the generations to come. Through the study of Vyākaraṇa, Śabdas, which can express meaning and produce Dharma, can be known.

Notes : The construction of Vyākaraṇa is two-fold :- 1. The author does not pronounce the Śabda, he wishes to analyse, rather compose a Sūtra, that would be applicable to both the Śabda, he has in mind as well as many other similar Śabdas. So, those Śabdas (examples), which fall within the purview of the meaning of the Sūtra are perfected. The Sūtra is built in such a way that it is free from defects such as partial inapplicability (or Avyāpti), and over applicability (or Ativyāpti). For instance, 'iko yaṇaci' (Pāṇini. 6-1-77). 'Ik', when followed by ac, is replaced by yaṇ - this is the Sūtrārtha (meaning of the Sūtra). 'Dadhi + atra = dadhyatra (curd is here) etc. are examples.

2. In the second type the very Śabdas are pronounced in the Sūtra. Example: - Kaskādiṣu ca (Pāṇini- 8-3-48). 'Kaska etc. Śabdas, enumerated by Pāṇini in Kaskādigaṇa are fit for usage' - this is the meaning of the Sūtra. In some examples sakāra, and in some other ṣakara is applicable. Kaskaḥ, sapiṣkuṇḍikā, dhanuṣkapālam etc. are some examples where the present Sūtra is applicable.

Intro : Having established that since it is a Smṛti, Vyākaraṇa is an authority, the author explains *the difference between Śruti and Smṛti* –

अनादिमव्यवच्छिन्नां श्रुतिमाहुरकर्तृकाम् ।
शिष्टैर्निबध्यमाना तु न व्यवच्छिद्यते स्मृतिः ।।

145. anādimavyavacchinnām śrutimāhurakartṛkām
śiṣṭairnibadhyamānā tu na vyavacchidyate smṛtiḥ

Sum : The Veda is described as beginingless, authorless and endless. So far as the Smṛti is considered it is composed by Śiṣṭas, and is not interrupted.

Com : Vedas have emanated from the four faces of Brahma spontaneously. They are immortal. Vedas are not produced. They have nothing to do with Deluge, or the beginning of Yuga. The phonemes, words and accents would never change.

Smṛtis are not like that. They are built by sages. They are uninterrupted like an everflowing stream and therefore considered to be immortal.

Intro : The author has described the difference between Śruti and Smṛti in verse 145, from the point of view of Pūrvamīmāmsakas, who do not believe in Deluge or Pralaya. In this verse, he describes *the difference in accordance with those who believe in Deluge, i.e., Vedāntins* (or Uttaramīmāmsakas) –

अविभागाद्विवृत्तानामभिख्या स्वप्नवच्छ्रुतौ ।
भावतत्वं तु विज्ञाय विज्ञेभ्यो विहिता स्मृतिः ।।

146. avibhāgādvivṛttānāmabhikhyā svapnavacchṛtau
bhāvatattvam tu vijñāya vijñebhyo vihitā smṛtiḥ

Sum : In the beginning there was the Śabda in a single form without divisions. After Deluge, Ṛṣis were born out of Śabda. Human beings look things during the course of dream without the help of eyes or ears through mental process. Similarly, the Ṛṣis, can have the knowledge of Vedas without teaching.

At the beginning of Yuga, Vedas are born out of the exhalation of Parameśvara. They perish during Deluge. Deluge or Pralaya is acceptable to Śāstra (Vyākaraṇa). Smṛtis are built in accordance with Vedic tradition.

Notes : This verse holds the authority of Vedas following the Uttaramīmāmsā-darśana (Vedānta), which advocates the theories of Creation and Deluge (Sṛṣṭi and Pralaya).

Intro : Having given the picture of Śruti and Smṛti, the author *compares Vyākaraṇa with other Smṛtis –*

कायवाग्बुद्धिविषया ये मला समवस्थिताः ।
चिकित्सालक्षणाध्यात्मशास्त्रैस्तेषां विशुद्धयः ।।

147. kāyavāgbuddhiviṣayā ye malā samavasthitāḥ
cikitsālakṣaṇādhyātmaśāstraisteṣām viśuddhayaḥ

Sum : Whatever impurity there exists of the body, of the Śabda and of the mind, their purification is effected through the sciences of Carakasamhitā, Mahābhāṣya and Yogānuśāsana, respectively.

Com : Due to the change of the food consumed, place, time and situation one would become ill. In order to be comfortable one employs incorrect Śabdas and thus the speech would become defective. One's mind becomes defective due to illusion, deceit, accident/mistake, favour, grudge, lust etc.. The defects are generally called-malas. These defects pollute the mind/thinking and therefore such a mind cannot have the real picture of the object.

In order to get rid of the diseases one has to study Medical Treatises like Caraka & Suśruta and follow the instructions. Such a purpose is served through Vaidyaśāstra (or Medical works). In order to get rid of the mental defects one has to study the Yogānuśāsana (work on transcendental matters) and practise. That is the purpose of Yogaśāstra.

Similarly, Vyākaraṇa purifies one's defects of speech. The incorrect Śabdas themselves are the defects of Speech. Thus, like other Smṛtis, Vyākaraṇa also serves a useful purpose.

Patañjali is said to have written three works, viz. Pātañjala-yogadarśanam, Vyākaraṇamahābhāṣyam and Carakasamhitā, in order to help the people get rid of the blemishes related to Manovākkāya (mind, speech and body)- this is the essence of this verse.

Intro : Having until now expalined that Sādhuśabdas are the cause of Dharma, the author is going to talk *about the Asādhuśabdas, which are not fit to use –*

शब्दः संस्कारहीनो यो गौरिति प्रयुयुक्षिते।
तमपभ्रंशमिच्छन्ति विशिष्टार्थनिवेशिनम्।।

148. śabdaḥ saṃskārahīno yo gauriti prayuyukṣite
tamapabhraṃśamicchanti viśiṣṭārthaniveśinaṃ

Sum : The ungrammatical form (for instance 'goṇī')' which is employed to denote a particular object, when (a correct form, for instance) 'gauḥ' is required to be used, is considered as a currupt form.

Com : The Śabdas, other than those, to which grammatical applications are instituted in Vyākaraṇa, are Asādhuśabdas–for instance, the Śabda 'gauḥ' is described as a correct one in Vyākaraṇa. If the Śabda is not employed in accordance with the Vyākaraṇa applications, then it would be an Asādhuśabda-gāvī, goṇī, gotā, gopotalikā etc. These Śabdas are Asādhus, in the sense of a cow. Among them 'goṇī' and 'gotā' are Sādhus in another sense (a gunny bag and the quality of cowness respectively). This will be clear in verse 149.

Intro : In the earlier verse it is said that Apabhraṃśa (Asādhuśabda) is that which is used in a particular sense (viśiṣṭārthaniveśinam-employed in a particular sense). The implication is that *the same Śabda is apabhraṃśa in a particular sense, and sādhu in another sense.* This concept in being illustrated–

अस्वगोण्यादयः शब्दाः साधवो विषयान्तरे।
निमित्तभेदात्सर्वत्र साधुत्वं च व्यवस्थितम्।।

149. asvagoṇyādayaḥ śabdāḥ sādhavo viṣayāntare
nimittabhedātsarvatra sādhutvam ca vyavasthitam

Sum : Śabda like 'asva' and 'goṇī' are correct forms, when used to denote other objects (other than a horse and cow respectively). Correctness is Everywhere determined on the basis of what meaning a Śabda is to convey.

Com : The Śabda 'aśva' in the sense of a horse is sādhu, since it is employed in accordance with 'aśvatvajāti' (i.e. aśvatvajāti is the pravṛttinimitta-cause of the usage). Therefore, the Śabda 'asva' is not Sādhu in that sense. It is Sādhu in the sense of 'poor man' (na + sva = no-money-one who has no money-Bahuvrīhi-samāsa). Here in this context the Śabda functions in accordance with non-existence of money (dhanābhāva is the pravṛttinimitta). The Śabda is not absolutely Asādhu.

The Śabda, 'gauḥ', denotes cow and ray in accordance with gotvajāti. 'Goṇī' is Asādhu in that sense. 'Goṇī' is Sādhu in the sense of ' gunny bag', used generally to store rice etc.

'Gotā' is Asādhu in case it is used as a synonym to 'gauḥ'. The same is Sādhu to denote 'cowness' (gotā-gorbhāvaḥ-Taddhita suffix 'tal' in Bhāva).

The above Śabdas are Asādhus in a particular sense, but Sādhus in another sense. This is the idea behind the term 'viśiṣṭārthaniveśinam', employed by the author in verse 148.

Notes : In Sanskrit the Śabda 'Mitra' is there in masculine as well as neuter gender-Mitraḥ means the Sun, and Mitram means a friend. Both these Śabdas are Sādhus in the above mentioned form and meaning. There are many Śabdas of this type.

So much so that those Śabdas, which are far from Vyākaraṇasamskāra, irrespective of the meaning they denote are Asādhus. For example-Śarvaryām bhavam = Śārvarikam (which exists during night) is a correct one and Śārvaram is an incorrect one.

Intro : It was proposed in the last three verses that the Apabhramśas also denote meaning, but they are not Sādhus. Consequently, the author gives *the argument of Naiyāyikas* (logicians) by five verses –

ते साधुष्वनुमानेन प्रत्ययोत्पत्तिहेतवः ।
तादात्म्यमुपगम्येव शब्दार्थस्य प्रकाशकाः ।।

150. te sādhuṣvanumānena pratyayotpattihetavaḥ
tādātmyamupagamyeva śabdārthasya prakāśakāḥ.

Sum : These incorrect forms cause the comprehension of the meaning of the correct forms through recollection of correct forms. They apparently identify themselves with the correct forms and convey the meaning.

Com : The Apabhramśas are born out of Sādhuśabdas. The Asādhuśabdas cannot denote meaning,. There is no capacity (Śakti) in them. Only Sādhuśabdas are Śaktas (have the capacity to denote the meaning). Only Śaktaspada is Sādhu. When an incorrect Śabda is uttered then the related Sādhuśabda is recollected and that Sādhuśabda only can denote the meaning. The feeling of identity or Tādātmya is due to the similarity of Asādhuśabda with Sādhuśabdā this is the viewpoint of Naiyāyikas.

Intro : The author refers to the *Naiyāyika-theory* –

न शिष्टैरनुगम्यन्ते पर्याया इव साधवः ।
ते यतः स्मृतिशास्त्रेण तस्मात्साक्षादवाचकाः ।।

151. na śiṣṭairanugamyante paryāyā iva sādhavaḥ
te yataḥ smṛtiśāstreṇa tasmātsākṣādavācakāḥ

Sum : Because these incorrect forms are not accepted by Śiṣṭas as well as the Vyākaraṇaśāstra, as valid synonyms (of the correct forms), they are not capable of expressing the meaning directly.

Com : This verse clarifies the following doubt-why the incorrect forms are not considered as synonyms alongwith the correct synonyms ? In case, they are, they would also be expressive. The Śiṣṭas have not employed these Śabdas alongwith the Sādhuśabdas. Nor the Vyākaraṇaśāstra has analysed the same. In case, the Asādhuśabdas are also expressive, the Śiṣṭas would have used them alongwith other synonyms. The Vyākaraṇa too would have analysed by showing the formation, i.e. root-suffix etc. Since neither had happened, it is certain that they are not expresssive.

Notes : Therefore, they do not express the meaning directly. They make the relevant Sādhuśabda recollected, and through that express the meaning.

Intro : The author illustrates the concept (verse 150) that the *Sādhuśabda is recolleced through the Asādhuśabda*, and thus the latter expresses the meaning –

अम्बाम्बेति यथा बाळः शिक्षमाणो प्रभाषते।
अव्यक्तं तद्विदां तेन व्यक्तो भवति निश्चयः ।।

152. ambāmbeti yathā bālaḥ śikṣamāno prabhāṣate
avyaktam tadvidām tena vyakto bhavati niścayaḥ

Sum : When a boy, who is being instructed, indistinctly utters 'ambā' 'ambā'...those who know the correct form understand it through the indistinct one (connected with the next verse).

Com : A child of one or two years old is trained in the pronunciation of Śabdas Due to lack of vigour the child's pronunciation is unclear. The elders infer the real Śabdas and understand the child's language and not directly.

Intro : The same concept is being *substantiated* –

एवं साधौ प्रयोक्तव्ये योऽपभ्रंशः प्रयुज्यते।
तेन साधुव्यवहितः कश्चिदर्थोऽभिधीयते।।

153. evam sādhau prayoktavye yo 'pabhramśaḥ prayujyate
tena sādhuvyavahitaḥ kaścidartho 'bhidhīyate

Sum : Similarly, the meaning conveyed by a correct form is conveyed by an incorrect form, which is used where the correct one ought to be.

Com : Only Sādhuśabda can express the meaning. In case an Asādhuśabda is used, where a Sādhuśabda ought to be, then the former would not render the meaning. It rather makes the hearer recollect the related Sādhuśabda and through that the meaning is achieved. The Śabdas of a child are an example.

Notes : The concept quoted in verse 150 is elaborated in verses-152 & 153.

Intro : It is not applicable in every case that when an Asādhuśabda is pronounced, the Sādhuśabda is recollected and the meaning is comprehended, as we find people, who do not have the knowledge of Sādhuśabdas speak to each other. They convey their ideas to each other without difficulty.-in response to this question the author *elaborates the meaning of the second part of verse 150*, i.e. 'tādātmyamupagamyeva śabdārthasya prakāśakāḥ' –

> पारम्पर्यादपभ्रंशा विगुणेष्वभिधातृषु ।
> प्रसिद्धिमागता येषु तेषां साधुरवाचकः ।।

154. pāramparyādapabhramśā viguṇeṣvabhidhātṛṣu
prasiddhimāgatā yeṣu teṣām sādhuravācakaḥ

Sum : Where they are in use, forms which have become current among currupt speakers (due to abnormal condition of speech-organs) from generation to generation, in such cases the correct form is not the one which conveys the meaning.

Com : After the speech-organs like teeth etc. start decaying the pronunciation would not be clear. Different phonemes are pronounced, or the pronunciation would not be clear-and such defects do crop up. Like thus the very form of the Śabda will change. When people with defective speech-organs pronounce certain Śabdas the listners would mistake the same for perfect ones. Such Asādhuśabdas itself would express the meaning. The recollection is not necessary.

Also, some people, rather most people, carry on transactions with Asādhuśabdas and they do not have the slight knowledge of Sādhuśabdas. In their case also the meaning is understood without the need of recollection of Sādhuśabdas.

Intro : Right form verse 150 till now the author has given the views of Naiyāyikas regarding the expression of meaning through Apabhramśas and hereafter he *gives the classification of Sādhuśabdas and Asādhuśabdds in accordance with the theory of Vaiyākaraṇas* –

> दैवी वाग् व्यवकीर्णेयमशक्तैरभिधातृभिः ।
> अनित्यदर्शिनां त्वस्मिन् वादे बुद्धिविपर्ययः ।।

155. daivy vāg vyavakīrneyamaśaktairabhidhātṛbhiḥ
anityadarśinām tvasmin vāde buddhiviparyayaḥ

Sum : This devine Speech (Samskṛtam) has been intermixed with incorrect forms by incompetent speakers. Those who hold the view that the Śabda is non-eternal (for instance the Naiyāyikas) hold a contrary view on this.

Com : During earlier times people were pure (without defects like untruth and incapacity). As the time passed on they became subject to all types of defects. Their Speech too became polluted with Apaśabdas. Thus genuine language got mixed with Apabhramśas.

Naiyāyikas opine that-Śabda is not eternal. Sādhuśabdas do not produce any Dharma. They are simply useful in the expression of meaning. Initially there were only Asādhuśabdas. They were refined (Samskāra) and we got the Sādhuśabdas. Now when we pronounce Asādhuśabdas, then the Sādhuśabdas are recollected and the meaning is comprehended.

The term 'buddhiviparyayaḥ' insinuates that the concept of Naiyāyikas is not authoritative.

Intro : Both Sādhuśabdas and Asādhuśabdas are independent. They do not have any mutual relation such as 'prakṛti-vikṛti-bhāva'. Also *both are being inherited* – the author clarifies his point of view–

उभयेषामविच्छेदादन्यशब्दविवक्षया ।
योऽन्यः प्रयुज्यते शब्दो न सोऽर्थस्याभिधायकः ।।

156. ubhayeṣāmavicchedādanyaśabdavivakṣayā
yo'nyaḥ prayujyate sabdo na so 'rthasyābhidhāyakaḥ

Sum : Even according to the view that there is no difference between correct and incorrect forms (as held by the upholders of the doctrine of the non-eternal-Śabda, or Naiyāikas), a word used with the intention of using some other word, does not convey the meaning of the latter.

Com : The purport is that the theory of Naiyāyikas (the meaning of Apaśabda is understood through the recollection of related Sādhuśabda) is improper.

Index of Verses

Glossary

1. अंगिरस् (21) : Name of the clan of Ṛṣis who discerned and propagated Atharvaveda. Here it means Atharvaveda.

2. अथर्वन् (21) : Name of the clan of Ṛṣis who discerned and propagated Atharvaveda. Here it means Atharvaveda.

3. अध्याहित (3) : (synonym of Avyāhata), Superimposed, considered to be existing (although it does not exist).

4. अनवस्थित (106) : Recurring without break.

5. अनिबन्धन (138) Baseless; dry logic; immaterial.

6. अनुकार (5) : Reflection.

7. अनुतन्त्र (23) : A Śāstrīya treatise which follows another Śāstrīya treatise. The Vārtikas are an Anutantra of Pāṇini's Aṣṭādhyāyī.

8. अन्वाख्येय (24) : A Śabda that can be derived and analysed. In usages like 'anvākhyeyāḥ Śabdāḥ' it means fit for use, correct etc.

9. अपभ्रंश (148, 153, 154) : A Sādhu-Śabda that has undergone changes that are grammatically unacceptable. In spite of its incorrectness, when such a word is used then the genuine form of the same is recollected and the meaning is understood.

10. अपवर्ग (14) : Salvation, relief from (worldly) bindings.

11. अपोद्धार (24) : Separation. This term is used in the sense of separation of Prakṛti from Pratyaya and vice versa (apa + ud + dhāra).

12. अभिख्या (146) : Cognition, Jñāna.

13. अर्थप्रवृत्तितत्व (13) : A desire to say (Vivakṣā); the idea behind the usage of certain term/word.

14. अर्थवाद (8) : A write-up for a specific purpose. Some sentences in Vedas are neither injunctions nor censures. Either commendation of the In-

junctions (Vidhis) or condemnation of the Censures (Niṣedhas) is the purpose of these sentences. Such sentences are construed alongwith the injunctive or censuring sentences (See-Vidhinātvekavākyatvāt stutyarthena vidhīnām syuḥ-1-2-1-7 Mīmāmsādarśana of Jaimini, Anandasram, Puna, 1930, also chapter 1, Mahāvākyavicāraḥ, Dr K Subrahmanyam, 1986). Example-Vāyavyam śvetamālabheta bhūtikāmaḥ (Vidhi)-Vāyurvai kṣepiṣṭhā devatā, Vāyumeva svena bhāgadheyenopadhāvati...(Arthavāda)-Taittirīyasamhita 2-1-1, Vaidikasamśodhakamaṇḍal, Puna 1972.

15. अवग्रह (91) : Cognition (Jñāna); form of cognition.

16. अविभाग (128) : to be without parts.

17. अविवक्षा (137) : Having no desire to say anything; indifference.

18. आगम (27, 30, 133) : Uninterrupted tradition, (41) the custom inherited through uninterrupted tradition, the Śāstra-treatise which keeps up the uninterrupted tradition.

19. आण्डभाव (51) : to be as important as the fluid in the core of the egg.

20. आत्मन् (17) : Ātmā (Soul), the minutest noumenon.

21 आम्नात (2) : The thing described as an authority in śāstras.

22. आसन्न (11) : The nearest one.

23. इतिकर्तव्यता (122) : The worldly transaction; the thinking/cognition that such a work has to be done like this; knowledge of doing things.

24. उपादानशब्द (44) : The Śabda which directly gives the meaning. Upādāna means the original cause. Since it superimposes meanings in itself and also due to the association with the word 'Śabda, the term means 'Vācaka (expressor). The primary meaning is— in regard with Śabdas, which are Vācakas.

25. कम्प (107) : The vibration produced due to the touch of vocal cords by air at the time of utterance.

26. करणविन्यास (123) : The employment of speech organs in the utterance of Śabdas.

27. क्रतु (51) : One which makes—is the derivative meaning. Mind (Buddhi). An internal capacity that causes the manifestation of Śabdas.

28. क्रियापद (114) : A verbal form derived from a root (dhātu) and fit for usage. Example-bhavati (bhū), pacati (pac). Dhātu is different from kriyāpada. A Dhātu cannot be used independently (na kevalā prakṛtiḥ prayoktavyā napi

pratyayaḥ-neither a root, i.e. dhātu/prātipadika, nor a suffix can independently be used – Mahābhāṣya).

29. गुण (62, 64) : The thing which is used/desired to be used with secondary importance. In Nyāyadarśana 24 Guṇās (Rasa, Gandha etc.) are described. They are not taken in this context.

30. ग्राह्य (55) : The thing that can be conceived through the mind immediately after a Śabda is uttered. A Śabda is used with regard to a thing and the same thing is Grāhya. The instrument in the conception, i.e. Buddhi etc, is Grāhaka.

31. छन्दस्य (17) : 'A group of Vedic Mantras' – is the derivative meaning. The Ātmā, proposed by such a group is also Chandasya.

32. ज्ञान (86) Intelligence; Cognition; Knowledge.

33. तर्क (30, 43, 136, 138) : To decide certain thing with the help of Anumāna and Upamāna. Such a decision should not be contrary to Śāstra or Pratyakṣa. According to Naiyāyikas' terminology Tarka is Vyāpakāropa through Vyāpyāropa – if fire would have not been there the smoke would also have not been (Here-Vyāpya is Vahni and Vyāpaka is smoke).

34. त्रयी (133) : The trio of Vedas, viz. Ṛk, Yajus, and Sāma. Theists believe that these are works of impersonal origin (apauruṣeya) or Īśvarajanya (born from Īśvara).

35. धर्म (31, 140) : 1. The sacred duty ordained by Śāstra; a quality in a thing (ex. greatness).

36. नादं (102) : Sound. Due to the change/difference in sound the changes/differences in vowels. i.e. hrasva, dirgha and pluta, and slowness and fastness in utterance take place.

37. निबन्धन (13) : The root cause/base. In both the senses Bhartṛhari used both the words, i.e. nibandhanam and nibandhanā. at several places.

38. पद (71, 72, 73) : A part of a sentence in the form of noun or verb. A (meaningfull) group of letters.

39. पदस्थान (16) : Step.

40. परमात्रा (129) : To shine with another form.

41. पश्यन्ती (143) : One of the four types of Vāk (the others being Parā, : Madhyamā and Vaikhary). In accordance with the desire it transforms into ordinary Vāk. It is situated at the navel (Paśyantī nābhisamsthitā).

42. पारार्थ्य (137) : The quality of being meant for causing somethingelse.

43. पुराणगाः (45) : The commentators of Purāṇas. Those who follow the philosophical doctrines proposed in Rāmāyaṇa, Mahābhārata etc.

44. प्रकर्ष (64) : The superiority of qualities. This would help in application of suffixes, 'tarap' and 'tamap' (ex. śuklataraḥ-whiter/śuklatamaḥ-whitest).

45. प्रक्रिया (1) : Formation; process of formation; defining the form.

46. प्रणव (9) : Omkāra (omkārapraṇavau samau-Amarakośa). This is the essence of Vedas.

47. प्रतिपत्ति (79) : Cognition; Jñāna.

48. प्रतिपादक (24) : The root, i.e. a dhātu/prātipadika, upon which no vibhaktipratyaya is applied, but meaningful. It is not fit for usage.

49. प्रविभाग (128) : The transformation of Śabdabrahman into different things in the Universe. The same is also called Jāgradavasthā of Śabdabrahman.

50. प्राप्यकारिन् (80) : That which functions after touching certain thing. Ex.Eye. It generates cognition after coming in touch with an object.

51. बीज (84) : The hidden capacity; a seed.

52. ब्रह्मन् (11, 22) : The noumenon proposed in Vedas. The same is the essence of Vedas and also called Śabdabrahman.

53. मूर्तिव्यापारदर्शनम् (19) : Observation of the functions of the visible things in the Universe.

54. लैंगिकी (137) : Known through a Śabda with hidden meaning. The cognition that is achieved through the knowledge of a distinctive quality in an object.

55. वाक् (124, 127) : The audible speech. Not only Vaikhary but also the earlier forms, viz. Madhyamā and Paśyantī are called 'Vāk'. Some scholars have accepted the name even for the earliest form called 'Parā'.

56. विकार (3) : Form ; transformation ; change.

57. विद्या (10) : The Śāstrīya appliction.

58. विधाता (10) : The Creator ; organiser.

59. वृत्ति (51, 75) : The state where certain qualities are produced and others perish.

60. वृद्धि (59) : 'Ā, ai and au' are called Vrddhi in Vyākaraṇaśāstra.

61. वेद (5) : Veda. It is the form of Śabdabrahman.

62. वैकृत (19, 77) : That, connected with the transformed thing. Vaikṛtadhvanis cause the Vṛttis, viz. Druta, Madhya and Vilambita. After the Sphoṭaśabda is manifested, the Vaikṛtadhvanis keep it ringing for some time. They won't cause any difference in the Sphoṭaśabda.

63. वैखरी (143) : The Śabda that is audible. It is one of the four Vāks (see 55 above).

64. व्यक्ति (68, 69) : A thing/an object; a person.

65. व्यंजन (116) : To make clear; manifestation, causing the generation of certain thing in the way a fan indicates the existence of air.

66. व्यवस्थानित्यता (28) : The quality of having changes in the form at surface level but without any difference in the core.

67. व्याकरण (11, 13, 22, 142) : The Śāstra which decides the Sādhu-Śabdas etc.

68. शब्द (1, 107, 108, 111, 112) : Generally it means sound. It is applied to all the stages of utterance. Unclear sound, clear sound, meaningful clear sound (word etc), sound that is not audible, mental capacity that causes sound, the Śabdabrahman that causes all transactions – these are all different stages of Śabda. It is used in the sense of root, suffix, phoneme, morpheme, word, sentence, discourse, Parā, Praśyantī, Madhyamā, and Vaikhary (it is an untrannslatable word. The rendering – 'Word' – with 'W' in capital-offered by some translators does not convey all the meanings and therefore I rather adopted the word in this work. There is no othergo but to decide the meaning according to the context).

69. शब्दतत्व (1) : Śabdatattva is the prominent capacity of a Śabda. Śabdabrahman, Nādabrahman and Sphoṭa are synonyms of the same (The Vigraha can be either शब्दस्य तत्तवम् or शब्दः तत्वमस्य

70. शब्दधर्म (58) : Two qualities of Śabda, i.e. to comprehend the meaning and to express the meaning (see 56 commentary).

71. शब्दार्थसम्बन्ध (23) : The relation of Śabda with Artha. Vaiyākaraṇas (Mīmāmsakas also) think that this relationship is eternal.

72. शिष्ट (27, 29) : Pundits with good culture ; those who have studied Vyākaraṇa etc. and who can explain the things therein : (Mahābhāṣya 6-3-109). शिष्टा वैयाकरणाः शास्त्रपूर्विका हि शष्टिः, वैयाकरणाश्च शास्त्रज्ञाः

73. संज्ञा (56, 66) : Name; terminological word; an artificial name; people know well through this (सम्यक् जानन्ति अनया) -is the derivation of this word-so anything that is instrumental in knowing is called Samjñā. It is common

in common parlance as well as Śāstra (in verse 126 the word denotes the Conciousness in the beings).

74. संज्ञिन् (59, 66) : A thing/ object that is dentoed by a Samjñā.

75. संनिपात (109) : A kind of process.

76. संस्कार (79) : To improve the capacity/to make fit in order to fulfil the task.

77. समाम्नात (5) : That is pronounced authoritatively.

78. सायुज्य (131) : Union.

79. सिद्धि (36) : Fulfilment of the desired thing.

80. सोढत्व (82):: To bear in mind; commit to heart by recitation.

81. स्फोट (49, 75, 77, 81, 93, 102, 103, 106) : That which makes things clear; the eternal Śabda;(स्फुटति अर्थः अस्मात् इति स्फोटः meaning becomes clear by this-throu; this derivation the Sabda that dentoes the meaning is Sphoṭa (an untranslatable word). Vaiyākaraṇas believe that Sphoṭa is in the form of Madhyamā.

82 स्मृति (7, 145) : The traditional, inherited and authoritative sentence.

83. स्वमात्रा (129) : Own existence; own form

84. हेतुवाद (41) : Argument preceded by reasoning.

Bibliography

Bhartṛhari — Vākyapadīya

(a) Kāṇḍas 1&2 with Ambākartrī, Sampūrṇānanda Sanskrit Uni. Varanasi 1986

(b) Kāṇḍas 1&2 Engl. trans. by Raghavan Pillai Motilal, Delhi, 1971.

(c) Kāṇḍa 3 (Helārāja com.) Ed. KAS Iyer, Deccan college, Poona, 1963.

(d) Brahmakāṇḍa (Vṛtti of Bhartṛhari) Ed. KAS Iyer, Deccan College, Poona, 1966.

(e) Brahmakāṇḍa, Com. by Suryanarayana Sukla, Chowkhamba, Varanasi, 1975.

(f) Kāṇḍas 1&2,. Telugu trans. Telugu Academy, Hyderabad (India) 1974.

(g) Padakāṇḍa, Telugu trans. Telugu Academy, Hyderabad (India) 1980).

Jaimini — Mīmāmsādarśanam, Anandasram Poona, 1930.

Nāgeśabhaṭṭa — Laghumañjūṣā, Chowkhamba, Varanasi, 1973.

Patañjali — Mahābhāṣyam (Pradīpodyta), Chowkhamba, Varanasi, 1981.

Yāska — Niruktam, Meharchand Laksmanadas (Varanasi ?) 1963.